Will the REAL MORMONS STAND UP *and* SOUND *the* ALARM?

VERN PORTER

Copyright © 2019 by Vern Duane Porter.

ISBN Softcover   978-1-950580-83-5

All rights reserved. No part of this book may be reproduced or transmitted in any form or by any means, electronic or mechanical, including photocopying, recording, or by any information storage and retrieval system without express written permission from the author, except in the case of brief quotations embodied in critical reviews and certain other non-commercial uses permitted by copyright law.

Printed in the United States of America.

To order additional copies of this book, contact:
Bookwhip
1-855-339-3589
https://www.bookwhip.com

CONTENTS

Disclaimer and Warning v
List of Abbreviations vii
Introduction ix

Chapter 1. Apostasy 1
Chapter 2. The Restoration 11
Chapter 3. Mormon Miracles 21
Chapter 4. Mormon Backsliding 28
Chapter 5. Nauvoo 46
Chapter 6. The Mormon Church Today 62
Chapter 7. My Personal Story 73
Chapter 8. My Mission 83
Chapter 9. Getting On With My Life 99
Chapter 10. To Hell and Back 112
Chapter 11. The Effort to Turn the Church into a Cult 122

DISCLAIMER AND WARNING

Because of my lack of mental and physical stamina, I must apologize for the quality of the editing. My fight with cancer has been expensive so I have decided to do the editing myself rather than further impose on my friends.

I am no longer an apostate as I have been re-baptized and confirmed a member of the Church of Jesus Christ of Latter-Day Saints after a 25 year absence from that church. My blessings have been restored so I am once again an Elder, I have a temple recommend, and I am active in my local ward.

My beliefs are my own and I am not a member of a secret group, nor do I wish to establish a following. I sustain Thomas S. Monson as the prophet and president of the Church. I believe that the general authorities need our prayers and deserve our good will even when we disagree with them.

I am writing this book as an objection to the failure of local members to respect my right to disagree with them on matters of speculation and the falsification of our history. There is no place in the church for a volunteer corps of self appointed Danites who believe that they have a right to persecute and ridicule those with whom they disagree. Members are adding speculation which has not be canonized to our list of official doctrine for the purpose of throwing their weight around and intimidating those who disagree with them.

This book contains criticisms of some of our past general authorities because I blame some of them for the bad behavior of local members and leaders. A misunderstanding of the scriptures has allowed some members and leaders to imagine that when they have an idea without their minds being darkened, they can consider the idea revelation.

The result is sometimes solid doctrine being replaced by fables. I'm suggesting that when our youth leave home and start thinking for themselves some of them learn to see through these fables and their testimonies are damaged.

Many names are being left out as this book may cause even my best friends to be embarrassed about knowing me in the current authoritarian environment of the Church. The names of those who have verbally abused me were left out in order to avoid having to listen to their denials.

LIST OF ABBREVIATIONS

List of abbreviations for the most frequently quoted sources

BM = The Book of Mormon

CHC = A Comprehensive History of the Church of Jesus Christ of Latter-Day Saints.

D&C = THE DOCTRINE AND COVENANTS of the LDS Church

HC = History of the Church of Jesus Christ of Latter-Day Saints

LDS Church = The Church of Jesus Christ of Latter-Day Saints

Mormons = Members of the LDS Church

The King James version of the Bible is used

INTRODUCTION

This book contains both the bitter and the sweet things I have to say about the Church of Jesus Christ of Latter-Day Saints, the Mormons. Serving a mission from March of 1961-March of 1963 was a life changing experience. However, several times a year I am reminded of the year I spent working with the Church's Boy Scout program in Chico, California about forty five years ago. The scout I remember best still calls me occasionally. He is married man and the father of several children most of whom have served on missions or will within a few years. He still calls me several times a year to tell me what a good influence I was in his life. When I was re-baptized several years ago he was there to welcome me back into the Church.

A lot has happened to me since I was born in Minnesota during the early 1940s. It was a part of the heartland marked by small farms, small towns, and small businesses. People there understood that their feelings of self-worth were bolstered by their success at providing for themselves and others. We didn't need a book to tell us that no man is an island for we were in the land of community barn raising and country doctors who waited until the harvest to collect payment for services rendered and the penniless widow who would pay with what she could spare from her garden or flock. Because government was so small and so far away people had incentives for sticking together and being concerned about each other.

I was born in a log farmhouse, in an area where Mormons were unknown and you had to travel far to find someone who wasn't descended from recent immigrants who had been born in northern Europe. By the time I was six years old we had left Minnesota for California without any memory on my part of any association with religion. When we were old enough to go to church without them our parents sent us (me and my two sisters) to the nearest church which was a Southern Baptist Church where I attended until I was eighteen. I became a Mormon (a member of the Church of Jesus Christ of Latter-Day Saints) when I was just out of high school. It changed my life and brought me renewed confidence in the goodness of God.

The Mormon doctrine about the barring of African blacks from the priesthood was somewhat of a mystery and it didn't dawn on me at first how limiting it was to be unable to be ordained, but the fact that Joseph Smith had ordained a black man was some consolation. Also, it never dawned on me that shortly after the church was organized unworthy people infiltrated even its leadership organizations and not all of them left the Church after sabotaging the effort to settle in Missouri. The desire to change the Church to make it more to their liking, strengthened them to endure even the horrible ordeal of crossing the plains to Utah sometimes in an untimely fashion and poorly equipped. Many lives were lost by some of the migrating groups. Their quest for personal power and influence in the affairs of the Church drove them to remain with the faithful.

Less than two years after joining the Church I was called to serve on a two year full time mission. The first two weeks were spent in the mission home in Salt Lake City. While there a black member of the Church bore his testimony to us. That helped to calm my concerns about discrimination in the Church. After serving my mission I attended Diablo Valley College near my home in California for several years where I became acquainted with an instructor who was doing a study on the attitudes of Mormons towards blacks for his Doctoral Thesis. It pleased me to find out his study showed that when Mormons were compared to non-Mormons of similar social/economic backgrounds, the results were similar. This gave me some satisfaction for a few years for I was concerned that the practice of refusing to ordain blacks might have resulted in more bigotry in the Church than in the general population of the nation.

About fifteen years later I became a member of a stake quorum of Seventy which meant I was a permanent, part-time missionary working for a living at a regular job. Soon I noticed an effort by some to make the Church a haven for racists. The Mormons who were racists would tell their racist friends, "You ought to join the Church, we know how to keep the blacks in their place." I was teaching the Investigator Class at that time so I told them, "I believe we are much too proud of the fact that blacks can't hold the priesthood. Their black skin is not the curse of Cain and they aren't poison to the temple for they can be baptized for the dead there."

As a result of the abuse I received over those remarks, I reexamined the old accusations against the Church by studying our histories, scriptures, and the record of conference talks from the early days in Utah instead of only our commentaries by Church leaders and scholars. Those early conference sermons are in a 26 volume set called the *Journal of Discourses*. I also had many long discussions with a knowledgeable member of the Church Institute Department in order to get some help in understanding inconsistencies in the teachings of the Church. I threw everything at him I could find in the scriptures, the *Journal of Discourses* and the Church histories and commentaries. He seemed to be familiar with all of them, but he didn't even try to explain them, he merely said "I know the Church is true".

It is my contention that the Church of Jesus Christ of Latter-Day Saints has on it's membership roles and among the leaders some people with personal agendas to advance doctrine not in keeping with the gospel of Jesus Christ as described in our scriptures. I have no plan or desire to weed them out as the Lord will see to it in his own due time. Because the Lord made it clear that He wants the wheat and tares to grow up together in the last days, I don't believe that He will ask his leaders here on earth to entirely weed out heretics. But, I do wish to call attention to some of the false doctrine and cover ups which remain an embarrassment and a danger because they give encouragement to polygamists, closet racists, and pious snobs in the church who occasionally attempt to chase those who don't agree with them, out of the Church. Every group, whether political, religious, or fraternal has fanatics in it who see enemies behind every disagreement and the LDS Church is no exception. It may be that we are especially vulnerable to this problem because we believe the canon of scripture is not full. We believe in modern day revelation.

The Latter-Day Saints are carrying such a burden of guilt over the death of Joseph Smith and their failure to settle Missouri that they will not stand for anyone accusing their leaders today as Joseph had been accused. Our leaders have learned to be tolerant of each other and are slow to admit that a head of the Church has given them false doctrine. So, unless there are exceptional circumstances, a leader's heresies will be tolerated. Above all else we must avoid a repetition of our past disunity.

So at least some of our scholars know that we have been given a falsified and incomplete history of the Church in our commentaries and lesson manuals and they are part of a conspiracy to hide the truth from us. Perhaps it is because they don't know how to explain it or are afraid to try. I suspect they are afraid to try because the Saints have been assured by some of our leaders that God would not let our prophet lead us astray. The Book of Mormon explains why that is false doctrine (Jacob 4:14). *The Journal of Discourses* contains the record of the false doctrine and good doctrine taught by Brigham Young and others.

At this point it is important to note that not only did the early Saints face a lot of mob violence, but the Governor of Missouri went so far as to swear out an extermination order against the Latter-Day Saints in the late 1830s. Perhaps the horrible hardships they endured were sufficient to cause them to be in denial about their history. On the other hand the court case brought against them by the Reorganized Church of Jesus Christ of Latter-Day Saints undoubtedly gave added incentive to be in denial.

Local leadership in the church is handled by unpaid clergy with temporary assignments, but they have a handbook to guide them in dealing with problems. The handbook and the guidance from the spirit which comes to humble servants of the Lord usually keeps things on an even keel when problems arise. However, when people feel threatened and leaders are mistaken about who their true friends are the handbook and the spirit can sometimes be tossed aside in favor of "good old boy networks", and self-appointed Danites (Danites will be explained later in the book). Local leadership did not do right by me in more than one stake of Zion.

In my anger and frustration over being misled about our history by our own leaders I left the Church for about 25 years. Because of the beautiful doctrine of Jesus Christ which is contained in the Book of Mormon and the teachings of Joseph Smith I wasn't ready to completely disassociate myself from the Mormon movement so I joined the Reorganized Church of Jesus Christ of Latter-Day Saints. I soon noticed that the Reorganized Church was displaying attitudes towards the Book of Mormon which didn't impress me so I left them after a couple of years.

I am back now and most of my LDS friends have received me with open arms. Some have not. An essay on Race and the Priesthood issued on December 6, 2013 clearly refutes historic arguments which justified racism and the withholding of the priesthood, but without acknowledging Brigham Young's insistence that the policy would not change during mortality. An abbreviated version of Brigham's beliefs was found in a speech he gave before the territorial legislature. The abbreviated version only mentioned that blacks would someday receive the priesthood, thus they could report that as they sought the revelation they were "aware of the promises made by the prophets and presidents of the Church who have preceded us". This subtle subterfuge has been seen by some as a signal to get tough with anyone who speaks the truth on the matter, and I have learned this the hard way.

After coming back to the LDS Church many years later, I attended a meeting where a black member of the Church was the speaker. Like many members of the church I didn't realize that there were any doubts in the minds of our leaders about withholding the priesthood from African Blacks for the whole of their mortal lives until I heard that brother speak. The quotation he gave us from President David O. McKay in 1954 was a complete surprise to me. By David O. McKay - 1954; "There is not now, and there never has been a doctrine in this church that the Negroes are under a divine curse, there is no doctrine in the church of any kind pertaining to the Negro. We believe we have a scriptural precedent for withholding the priesthood from the Negro. It is a practice, not a doctrine and the practice someday will be changed, and that is all there is to it." Taken from *David O. McKay & the Rise of Modern Mormonism* by Greg Prince & William Robert Wright, pp79-80. David O. McKay apparently believed that the fact of speculation becoming so popular that many thought it to be revealed truth did not make it so.

From the afore mentioned black member I learned that the leaders of the Church were not all in agreement on the idea that the blacks would never obtain the priesthood during their mortal lives and I became aware that I'd forgotten a basic tenet of the Gospel which proclaims the equality of believers. The equality of believers is clearly taught in the New Testament, the Book of Mormon and our book of Doctrine and Covenants. In my book I will tell you how racist doctrine gained the upper hand among the Latter-Day Saints and show you some of the other false doctrine promoted in the Church, some of it no longer acknowledged.

The saints had brought many problems upon themselves and they were scourged from city to city for their failures. When they sang "All is well, all is well", it was sang with a penitent spirit knowing that when they had been chastened the Lord would own them and bless them. They knew that the Lord chastises whom He loves. Today when we sing that song I sense something different is going on, perhaps not in every case, but there is a pronounced tendency towards the vanity which the Book of Mormon warns against. In 2nd Nephi it is referred to as being "at ease in Zion" and thinking, "All is well in Zion, yea, Zion prospereth." The Book of Mormon itself warns us against our failure to believe that part of the Nephite record which we have been given first as seen in 3Nephi 26:9-11;

9) "And when they shall have received this, which is expedient that they should have first, to try their faith, and if it shall so be that they shall believe these things then shall the greater things be made manifest unto them.
10) And if it so be that they will not believe these things, then shall the greater things be withheld from them, unto their condemnation.
11) Behold, I was about to write them, all which were engraven (sp) upon the plates of Nephi, but the Lord forbade it, saying: I will try the faith of my people."

Notice that they were to be tested to see if they believed the Book of Mormon. Mormons tend to describe their being scourged from city to city as being "tested and tried". The test was to see if they believed the Book of Mormon and being scourged from city to city was the punishment they were to receive for their disbelief and failure to be obedient. However, accepting punishment can also serve as a test. In September of 1832 the saints were told that the whole church was under condemnation, D&C 84:56-57;

> 56) "And this condemnation resteth upon the children of Zion, even all.
> 57) And they shall remain under this condemnation until they repent and remember the new covenant, even the Book of Mormon ..."

The Lord did not sustain them and fight their battles as they tried to settle in Ohio, Missouri, and Nauvoo because they were not faithful. June of 1834 in D&C 105:3&7, the Lord chastised the people, but not the leaders of the church.

> 2) "But behold, they have not learned to be obedient to the things which I required at their hands, but are full of all manner of evil and do not impart of their substance, as becometh saints, to the poor and afflicted among them;
> 3) And my people must needs be chastened until they learn obedience, if it must needs be, by the things which they suffer."

July of 1837 the apostles were warned in D&C 112:12-13,

> 12) "And pray for thy brethren of the Twelve, Admonish them sharply for my name's sake, and let them be admonished for all their sins, and be ye faithful before me unto my name.
> 13) And after their temptations, and much tribulations, behold, I, the Lord, will feel after them, and if they harden not their hearts, and stiffen not their necks against me, they shall be converted, and I will heal them."

The above revelation was given in Kirtland, Ohio. They were then in turn driven from Kirtland, from Missouri, and from Nauvoo. The account of their perseverance through the chastening they received because of their failures is awe-inspiring. The main body of saints finally settled in Utah while those who were not willing to receive the punishment decreed by the Lord and prophesied by Jeremiah (Jeremiah 17:5-6) remained behind in the hopes of escaping it. Settling in Utah found those who came west in need of being converted for there is a clear record of the delusions entertained by Brigham Young and others. I will document some that you may not have heard of. That they eventually made the desert to blossom is testimony to the fact that they were not entirely cast off because of some bad apples and their failure to believe the Book of Mormon. Volumes have been written by LDS scholars and leaders in an attempt to hide Brigham Young's delusions. Considering the slaughter which their predecessors had faced perhaps we can give them a little slack for their failure to be honest about some of the black marks on our history. But, the fact remains, we still have not yet received the translation of the rest of the plates of Nephi. Perhaps we do not yet believe enough of the Book of Mormon.

Among the Latter-Day Saints there is a subculture of members who insist we believe "all or nothing" when it comes to alleged revelation in the Church and for many members that includes conference talks as well as the standard works (the scriptures) of the Church. *The Journal of Discourses* is made up almost entirely of conference talks. Not all of our leaders or even all of those who believe it should be "all or nothing" are pious snobs. When I wrote the First Presidency to request the restoration of my blessings, I told President Monson that my testimony did not require me to believe that all of our leaders had been true to their callings and my testimony did not require me to believe that the *Pearl of Great Price* was completely credible. He then sent a member of the quorum of Seventy to restore my blessings. So, I can testify that President Monson is not a pious snob as some members and local leaders are.

Regarding the *Journal of Discourses*; the fact is that some of those sermons contain beliefs which can get you kicked out of the Church today. Since the announcement that the priesthood is available to men of all races we no longer hear Brigham Young's quotations about the blacks never receiving the priesthood during their mortal lives. How he must have resented the fact that Joseph Smith had ordained at least one Black man, so much for the "all or nothing" doctrine.

Perhaps the most basic falsehood promoted by the Church is the idea that, as Latter-Day Saints, we all believe the same thing, thus the title of this book, *Will the real Mormons stand up and sound the alarm*. The irony is that the only tests of orthodoxy in the Church are in a very small set of questions about beliefs and personal behavior which are asked during interviews for baptism and Temple Recommends, callings, etc. and in the 13 Articles of Faith. Many Latter-Day Saints will wonder, "what is he talking about?", for a large majority of the Saints may never be aware that my complaints are real. I suspect that the kind of Latter-Day Saints I'm complaining about are only found in little clusters here and there in the Church or perhaps the stake I live in is unique (not likely). Those who stay away from controversy can easily avoid the problems I have faced in the Church. But for me, ignoring the problem is not the answer.

As part of my effort to confront error and snobbery in the Church, I will present a condensed version of the history of the Church of Jesus Christ of Latter-Day Saints. Someone has to lead the way, expose the errors, and help them display true humility. I am willing to challenge the Latter-Day Saints to set an example. About one third of the contents of the book will consist of autobiographical material.

I didn't date during high school, but I did attend the Saturday night dances put on by the Church, after my conversion. My first year and three quarters was so busy that I felt ready to serve a mission and I received a call to serve for two years in the Southern States Mission. I went with a group from Martinez Ward to the last dance before I left on my mission and I met a beautiful red headed young lady from Concord. It became love at first dance for me. Full time missionaries are not allowed to date or even hug a female younger than our mothers, but even so missionaries have been known to fall in love in the mission field. Although I did complete my two year mission, with only two months to go on my mission I asked to be released and go home early. Was I just homesick or was it about my mixed feelings over the beautiful red headed lady back home in Concord, California and a raven haired beauty in the mission field? You decide after reading the book.

CHAPTER 1

APOSTASY

Much of the scriptural record is about the failure of Biblical peoples to live their religion. The Israelite's backsliding started as they left Egypt and entered the wilderness. Jeremiah 7:22-24 says,

> 22) For I spake not unto your fathers, nor commanded them in the day that I brought them out of the land of Egypt, concerning burnt offerings or sacrifices:
> 23) But this thing commanded I them, saying, Obey my voice, and I will be your God, and ye shall be my people: and walk ye in all the ways I have commanded you, that it may be well unto you.
> 24) But they harkened not, nor inclined their ear, but walked in counsels and in the imagination of their evil heart, and went backward, and not forward.

The Israelites became proud of their sacrifices and offerings so much that Samuel had to tell Saul in 1Sam. 15:22, Behold, to obey is better than sacrifice, and to hearken than the fat of rams. Saul had just offered sacrifices of animals they had taken from an enemy, which the Israelites were commanded to destroy, not sacrifice. For his arrogance, Saul was told that his kingdom would be taken from him. The Lord told the Israelites in Hosea 6:6, For I desired mercy, and not sacrifice; and the knowledge of God more than burnt offerings.

Today the emblems of the Sacrament - or the Eucharist, as many Christians call them, - take the place of the Israelite sacrifice as it serves as a reminder of the atonement Jesus offered. Today the Lord would be saying, "To obey is better than partaking of the wafer or bread, and to hearken than drinking the wine, or grape juice or water".

The apostle Paul said in a letter about the Law of Moses, Galatians 3:19, 24

> 19) Wherefore then serveth the law? It was added because of transgressions, ...
> 24) Wherefore the law was our schoolmaster to bring us unto Christ."

There are things which have been added to the Law of Moses which do not fall into the category of the highest order of instruction. Ezekiel made reference to such when he said in Ezekiel 20:24-25,

> 24) Because they had not executed my judgments, but had despised my statutes, and had polluted my Sabbaths, and their eyes were after their father's idols.
> 25) Wherefore I gave them also statutes that were not good, and judgments whereby they should not live;

We are judged by the law we have been given and that which has become socially acceptable. Thank the Lord for the principle of repentance. I don't feel it necessary to attempt a complete list of statutes that were not good, but allow me to start with the practice of divorce and continue with a short list the Savior gave in Matthew 5:31-48.

> 31) It hath been said, Whosoever shall put away his wife, let him give her a writing of divorcement:
> 32) But I say unto you, That whosoever shall put away his wife, saving for the cause of fornication, causeth her to commit adultery: and whosoever shall marry her that is divorced committeth adultery,

33) Again, ye have heard that it hath been said by them of old time, Thou shalt not forswear thyself, but shalt perform unto the Lord thine oaths:

34) But I say unto you, swear not at all; neither by heaven; for it is God's throne:

35) Nor by the earth; for it is his footstool: ...

37) But let your communication be, Yea, yea; Nay, nay: for whatsoever is more than these cometh of evil.

38) Ye have heard that it hath been said, An eye for an eye, and a tooth for a tooth:

39) But I say unto you, that ye resist not evil: but whosoever shall smite thee on thy right cheek, turn to him the other also,

40) And if any man shall sue thee at the law, and take away thy coat, let him have thy cloke also.

41) And whosoever shall compel thee to go a mile, go with him twain.

42) Give to him that asketh thee, and from him that would borrow of thee turn not thou away.

43) Ye have heard that it hath been said, thou shalt love thy neighbor, and hate thine enemy.

44) But I say unto you, love your enemies, bless them that curse you, do good to them that hate you, and pray for them which despitefully use you, and persecute you; ...

48) Be ye therefore perfect, even as your Father which is in heaven is perfect.

Another example is the practice of polygamy which is condemned in the Book of Mormon. Jacob 2:24-28,

24) Behold, David and Solomon truly had many wives and concubines, which thing was abominable before me, saith the Lord.

25) Wherefore, thus saith the Lord, I have led this people forth out of the land of Jerusalem, by the power of mine arm, that I might raise up unto me a righteous branch from the fruit of the loins of Joseph.

26) Wherefore, I the Lord God will not suffer that this people shall do like unto them of old.
27) Wherefore, my brethren, hear me, and hearken to the word of the Lord: For there shall not any man among you have save it be one wife; and concubines he shall have none;
28) For I, the Lord God, delight in the chastity of women. And whoredoms are an abomination before me; thus saith the Lord of Hosts.

Some have said that the law of Moses was harsh because it specified death for those who struck or reviled one of their parents. Dennis Prager's answer to that accusation is that the law put an end to parents killing their children because the child had to be taken before the council to be judged in the matter and stoned by the community if found guilty. According to Prager this gave them warning that children had rights so they didn't bring charges against their children.

God's relationship with the Israelites was a special one. They were not commissioned to go into the world and gather everyone to their God. They were to be examples to the rest of the world so that God could demonstrate through them that He blesses those who are righteous and punishes those who are wicked. The law they were given was only about their worthiness to be part of the earthly kingdom God had established for them.

Though some prophets who came after Moses spoke of the resurrection, the law of Moses did not promise it to them, which gave the Jewish aristocracy (the Sadducees) justification for denying that the principle of resurrection/immortality was a necessary belief.

Even after they had been given "statutes which were not good and judgments by which they should not live," Moses gave the Israelites a list of blessings they would receive for keeping his commandments. It was only a list of earthly blessings. In Deuteronomy, Chapter 8, the Israelites were told that if they kept the commandments, the statutes, and the judgments, to do them that the Lord would bless them, their crops and herds. He told them that the Lord would take all sicknesses away from them. They were told that He would put all the evil diseases of Egypt on those who hated them. The Israelites were told that the Lord would do to all those of whom they were afraid as He had done to Egypt. For those who were in the Israelites way the Lord promised to send the hornet among them until those who are left, and hide themselves from thee, be destroyed.

Sometimes those who speak of the requirements of the Law of Moses tend to get carried away with suggestions that the children of Israel needed to have constant reminders of their special relationship with God. They had a complex list of things which made them unclean requiring them to bathe and wash their clothing. Many of them can be viewed as helping the Israelites to have some responsibility in ensuring that they would not incur the sicknesses God promised they would avoid if they kept the commandments, statutes and the judgments they were obligated to follow.

In chapter 9 of Deuteronomy, the Israelites were told that it was not because of their righteousness that their enemies were to be destroyed and driven out, it was because of their enemies unrighteousness. Their enemies were those who inhabited their promised land and those who would interfere with their effort to obtain it. They had no mandate to go beyond their promised land and find more of the wicked to destroy because the Israelites were to enjoy peace if they were righteous. When they had a King over them the king was not to multiply horses to himself or wives or silver and gold according to Deuteronomy Chapter 17.

Because the Israelites provoked the Lord to anger so many times, they never did completely drive out the wicked who possessed their land. They cried unto the Lord when they were in trouble and forgot the Lord when they prospered, in other words they were normal people.

Eventually they became so wicked themselves that the Lord allowed them to be taken into captivity. They were warned in Deuteronomy Chapter 8 that when they had become wealthy they should not begin to think that their power and the might of their own hands was responsible for their success and forget the Lord lest they be destroyed. In Deuteronomy, the Israelites were told that the Lord led them in the wilderness in order to prove them and to know what was in their hearts. You might say that He was discovering their weaknesses and improving those who were able to stand the heat. Deuteronomy 8:2, "And thou shalt remember all the way which the Lord thy God led thee these forty years in the wilderness, to humble thee, and to prove thee, to know what was in thine heart, whether thou wouldest keep the commandments, or no."

While the leaders of the Jews were vassals to the Roman Empire they had become corrupt enough to condemn Jesus to death. This marked the end of the Mosaic Dispensation and the beginning of the Christian Era. Before they can fully enter into their latter-day glory they must do as they were told in Leviticus 26, they must confess their sins and the sins of their fathers.

The rejection and crucifixion of Jesus by the Jews marked the beginning of the fulfillment of God's promise to Abraham that in his seed shall all the nations of the Earth be blessed. Because of the rejection of Christ by the Jews the Gospel was taken too much of the known world. The new religion spread quickly and Christians became a true community of believers as they took steps to care for the spiritual and physical needs of the members. This new gospel which Jesus delivered was not as the Law of Moses, merely about earthly blessings. It was about eternal blessings in heaven and punishment in hell. The punishment could be either temporary or permanent.

The gospel which Jesus taught revealed a just God who had different amounts of punishment awaiting those who would be punished (Luke 12:47-48) and different degrees of glory according to their capacity to accept responsibility (see Matthew 25:14-30 and 1Cor.15:40-42). He made it clear that He would accept converts from their youth to their old age. Those who labored in the harvest starting in the strength of their youth would receive the same wages as those weren't called until the evening of their lives (Matthew 20:1-14). Apparently, that which constitutes wages and that which counts as responsibility do not fall into the same category.

Eventually, the inspired leadership of the twelve apostles was lost to the church as they were martyred without being replaced. The apostles had little motivation to continue the practice of replacing their departed brethren as there was widespread belief that the Savior's second coming was near at hand. Paul felt the need to tell the Thessalonians in 2nd Thes. 2:3, "Let no man deceive you by any means: for that day shall not come, except there come a falling away first, and that man of sin be revealed, the son of perdition:" It was not likely very many years later that another apostle warned the saints in a general epistle, 1John 2:18, "Little children, it is the last time: and as ye have heard that anti-Christ shall come, even now are there many anti-Christ; whereby we know that it is the last time." They made the mistake of associating the nearness of the apostasy with the second coming of the Lord.

Jesus proclaimed the fact that only the Father knows the time of the second coming. I believe it was to keep us all on our toes. To declare the exact time of the Lord's second coming would be to invite slothfulness on the part of those who lived at a time in which it was not expected. In the meantime, the Savior had declared mortality a probationary state by telling his followers that his kingdom was not of this world. With the passing of the apostles, the Christians drifted about with every wind of doctrine until they became linked to political movements and kingdoms. Faith in Jesus is a powerful thing which does not necessarily depend on membership in a particular church and history is full of accounts of those who resisted the power of politicized Christianity. Eventually God raised up men who would dare to establish a nation wherein secular government was not allowed to interfere with religion. Against all odds, a nation called the United States of America was formed by such men with God's help. This prepared the way for Joseph Smith to receive his mission from God.

As members of the Church of Jesus Christ of Latter-Day Saints, we believe that the commission Jesus gave his twelve apostles eventually expired as the quorum of twelve Apostles were killed off without being replaced. We believe that the commission to preach the gospel and perform the ordinances of salvation has been renewed to Joseph Smith and new apostles have been chosen and ordained. Up to a few years ago, I felt that the Latter-Day Saints had lost their commission to spread the gospel. Some very vivid dreams changed my mind and my testimony of the priesthood authority of the LDS Church was restored. My testimony no longer depends upon any church leader remaining true to his calling. The Children of Israel had their problems and so have we.

As an example of how badly things can go when the wrong philosophy wins out, let me briefly cite what was happening to mainstream Islam over a thousand years ago culminating in intellectual suicide eight centuries ago according to Robert R. Reilly in *THE CLOSING OF THE MUSLIM MIND*. Opposing philosophies were developing which would determine which direction Islam was to take. Eventually two schools of thought fought for predominance. The Ash'arites claimed that the Qur'an was not created, but has forever coexisted with Allah in eternity. The Mu'tazilites claimed that it came into existence as it was revealed. The Ash'arites worshiped a god of unrestrained will and power for whom the Qur'an, the sayings of Muhammad and other approved writings set the limits of our understanding of Allah and all approved knowledge. Things which were created were not created by Allah's intelligence, but by his will. It is therefore not acceptable to consider the hows and whys of things. It is not surprising then that the outlawing of Mu'tazilism put an end to the Islamic golden age of scientific advancement. The result of Sharia law and radical Islamic jihad is a very rigid, narrow reality with little room left for the rest of us to exist in without shackles.

So, did an angel give Muhammad instructions in that cave? I can picture father Abraham asking the Lord to send some help to his Arab descendants who were subject to the ignorance and superstition of idol worship. The record of those sessions in the cave gave Moslems instructions which made it possible for them to live in peace with their Christian and Jewish neighbors. The Koran gives wonderful support to moderate Islam. To the Moslem who feels he is being oppressed it says, "Was not Allah's earth spacious that ye could have migrated therein?" Surah IV verse 97.

To the Moslem who might be tempted by the promise of many virgins the Koran says, with regard to wedded bliss, "The provision of thy Lord is better and more lasting". Surah XX verse 131.

To the Moslem practicing Sharia law by performing an honor killing on a female of his family who had been raped or was merely associating with a stranger the Koran is a reminder that even adultery only requires a flogging. Surah XXIV verse 2.

To the promoter of radical jihad who insists that he no longer needs to believe parts of the Koran it says, referring to Allah, "He it is Who hath revealed unto thee (Muhammad) the Scripture wherein are clear revelations-They are the substance of the book-and others (which are) allegorical. But those in whose hearts is doubt pursue, forsooth, that which is allegorical seeking (to cause) dissension by seeking to explain it. None knoweth its explanation save Allah. And those who are of sound instruction say: We believe therein; the whole is from our Lord; but only men of understanding really heed." Surah III verse 7.

To the promoter of jihad who hates Jews and Christians the Koran says, "...For each we have appointed a divine and traced out way, had Allah willed He could have made you one community, but that He might try you by that which He hath given you (He hath made you as ye are). So vie one with another in good works, unto Allah ye will all return ... ." Surah V verse 48.

Sharia law and radical jihad are the refuge of a blood thirsty people, a cult of death. There is no place in society where we can be safe from them as they attempt to gain control. If Islam had only the Koran to guide them they would be much better off, but they also have reputed writings of Muhammad which they use to justify ignoring parts of their sacred scripture. It looks to me like Muhammad lost faith in the ability of his Arab brethren to learn from the Koran so he gave them "statutes by which they should not live and judgments which were not good" just as Moses did for the Israelites, only the Moslem version is much more harsh. The harshness of Sharia varies from sect to sect, but generally speaking it provides excuses for treating women as second class citizens, mutilating their genitalia and indulging in honor killings which are not the kind of behavior we would call honorable. I dare say that the Allah revealed in the Koran which I studied would not look kindly on those who practice Sharia.

When comparing the Israelite "statutes by which they should not live and the judgments which were not good" to the Islamic Sharia it is interesting to note that the Israelite's law merely created exceptions to the stricter code while Sharia promoted incentives for bloodthirsty behavior towards other peoples and oppressive attitudes towards their own women. Sharia promises virgins in the afterlife for murdering infidels, but the Israelites were told that having to kill their enemies was a punishment for them, the Israelites. The Lord would have chased their enemies out with hornets if they, the Israelites, had been righteous. This is quite a different narrative than the atheists like to give in their own accounts on the subject of the Israelites taking of their promised land. Exodus 23:28-30,

28) And I will send hornets before thee, which shall drive out the Hivite, the Canaanite, and the Hittite, from before thee.

29) I will not drive them out from before thee in one year; lest the land become desolate, and the beast of the field multiply against thee.

30) By little and little I will drive them out from before thee, until thou be increased, and inherit the land.

This promise was made before the Israelites had Aaron make a golden calf for them to worship and the Lord decreed that they should wander in the wilderness until a new generation grew up to inherit the promised land.

I am not an expert on Islam, but I'm happy to tell you that there is at least one Moslem people, the Kurds, who separate secular government from their religion and are happy to live in a democracy. This places them at risk from Islamic sects which promote Sharia. Moderate Moslems within the radical sects are also happy to live in a democracy. Those who favor Sharia and radical Jihad will only live in a democracy with hopes of gaining control of it. Where ever they are moderate Moslems fear speaking out against Sharia and radical Jihad lest they be declared heretics.

The Israelites were offered the opportunity to live a utopian dream as were the early Christians. Utopia is not easily obtained or held onto. The Children of Israel were promised a specific land, not the whole world, with no instructions to conquer the world. The early Christians were encouraged to proselytize the world, but not to establish an earthly kingdom which people were obligated to join. The Lord wants us to voluntarily serve him and love him and mortality is the time given us to choose one way or the other. Sharia is about forcing worship by the point of a sword if necessary.

CHAPTER 2

THE RESTORATION

We proclaim that we are organized to be the same church with the same gifts and blessings that Christ established while He was here on Earth as a mortal being. We are a church of miracles the same as the original was. Of the many miracles associated with the early days of the Church of Jesus Christ of Latter-Day Saints the most important and well known are the first vision and the coming forth of the Book of Mormon. It is no surprise that enemies of the Church tried to disprove both. A favorite attack on the Vision is the fact of several different versions having been given during the life of the prophet. The Book of Mormon was alleged to have been plagiarized from a novel.

I have read more than one version of the first vision in the past and found nothing troubling in them. Joseph eventually learned the value of keeping a journal, but failed to do so at first. We don't even have the date of the restoration of the Melchizedek Priesthood by angelic visitors as he and Oliver Cowdery had temporarily decided to keep it a secret because of the level of persecution existing at that time. Consideration of possible reactions to his account of the "first vision" may have influenced his recitation of the events depending on when and where the account was given. As a writer, I am well acquainted with the problem of the retelling of an event to different people at different times and places. We all vary in our ability to remember past events and different circumstances can result in the emphasizing of different aspects of an event. We also vary in our ability to recall in step by step sequence recent events or to logically connect related thoughts. My mother told me that when she wanted to know what had happened while she had been otherwise occupied she learned to ask my sisters because my accounts of what happened were often disjointed. It's something I still struggle with.

In the Journal of Discourses Vol. 7, page 243 Brigham Young is quoted as saying,

"... Brother Joseph ... revealed the will of the Lord to the people, and yet but few were really acquainted with Brother Joseph. He had all the weaknesses of a man when the vision was not upon him, when he was left to himself. He was constituted like other men, and would have required years and years longer in the flesh to become a Moses in all things."

When one is aware of Joseph's lack of education, it is no wonder some accused him of plagiarizing. Understanding the nature of the Book of Mormon, he translated and the revelations he received as compared to what came forth when he was left on his own leaves me with no concerns about the differing accounts of the first vision. One example will do for me. The Bible, the Book of Mormon, and the revelations in the D&C all clearly teach that the departed spirits go to separate places depending upon their righteousness. Yet when Joseph thought he knew something about the Greek and Hebrew languages he told the Saints gathered at the Nauvoo Temple that "the righteous and the wicked all go to the same world of spirits until the resurrection", page 425, *History of the Church*, Vol. 5, June 11th, 1843. He was not always in top form.

The account of the first vision in the Joseph Smith *History of the Church* (Vol. 1, pp. 5&6) and the most widely known version describes a fifteen year old Joseph alone in the woods, kneeling in prayer wanting to know which church to join. His prayer was interrupted by "some power which entirely overcame me, and had such an astonishing influence over me as to bind my tongue so that I could not speak." Before the Savior began his mortal ministry the Devil tempted him, but of course did not overpower him.

Satan's self-appointed mission is to tempt and challenge us. Before I left on my mission, the evil one showed me the power he has over those whose lust for power gets the best of them. A Bishop and a young man conspired to make a fool of me when the attendance records I was in charge of showed that the young man did not deserve the award he wanted and was about to be presented. I entered the mission field deeply scarred and distrustful of my leaders, but determined serve the Lord.

Joseph was delivered from his alarming situation by a pillar of light which descended upon him. "When the light rested upon me I saw two personages, whose brightness and glory defy all description, standing above me in the air." It was God and Jesus and they told Joseph to join none of the Churches.

Over the next few years, Joseph was given instructions by angelic messengers many times. Just a few months short of his 22nd birthday, in September of 1827 he obtained the Gold plates along with the Urim and Thummim. The Urim and Thummim consisted of two stones in silver bows and fastened to a breastplate. The history written on the gold plates was in a reformed Egyptian language and the Urim and Thummim allowed Joseph to see the Egyptian writing translated into English which he read for his scribe. The scribe read it back to Joseph who gave any corrections needed. This process was witnessed by several people and defies any non-miraculous explanation possible in the 1800s, thus it was translated by the "gift and power of God". The plates were obtained September 22nd of 1827, but because of numerous interruptions the translating was accomplished over a period of about two months from April to June of 1828.

When I came back to the Church after a 25 year absence, my wife and I attended a Church Institute of Religion class on the Book of Mormon. Not having read any background information on it for decades, I was amazed at the huge amount of supporting evidence available now. To supplement the information in the lesson manual I purchased a copy of *Echoes and evidences of the Book of Mormon* edited by Donald W. Parry, Daniel C. Peterson, and John W. Welch. Each of the dozen chapters had different authors and each was a testimony in and of itself.

The Book of Mormon starts out in Jerusalem with a prophet named Lehi and his family at the time of King Zedekiah shortly before the Babylonian captivity. Lehi's family and another family traveled for eight years in the wilderness of the Arabian peninsula before they settled down in an area with sufficient natural resources to build a ship to take them to the New World. In the third chapter of *Echoes and Evidences,* S. Kent Brown presents a wealth of information to verify the Book of Mormon account of the topography and names of places, information not available to Joseph Smith.

After building a ship they set sail for America and landed, it is thought, somewhere in the vicinity of Central America. There they eventually met up with a son of King Zedekiah and his party who had escaped the massacre in Jerusalem. They also discovered a man who was thought to be the last survivor of a great civilization which developed after the Lord brought a small group of them here from the time of the confounding of tongues in Babylon. In addition to that last survivor of a group of people from Tower of Babel times a written history of their journey to America and the civilization they established was obtained along with Urim and Thummim for translating it. This was the Urim and Thummim given to Joseph Smith for translating the Book of Mormon. In the 5th chapter of *Echoes and Evidences,* Donald W. Parry explains how the literary styles reveal Hebraisms and other ancient peculiarities relating to the cultures of the various inhabitants of the old world. The names of the people mentioned in the Book of Mormon show it to be culturally correct with regard to the two civilizations whose histories are recorded therein.

Of Lehi's family, one of his younger sons named Nephi was the first to take charge of recording their history. He also kept charge of the brass plates of Laban which contained as much of the Old Testament as had been kept up to that time by the Jews as well as some genealogies and writings of prophets from the Northern Kingdom. Large plates contained the secular history of the people and smaller plates the religious history. There were also the 24 plates of Ether who was the last prophet of the people from the Tower of Babel. Joseph Smith was given a condensed version of those histories, but two thirds of the plates were sealed and not to be translated until the Latter-Day Saints had been tested by the Lord. We are not to receive the greater things until we show the Lord that we believe that which Joseph was allowed to translate.

Our next major miracle involves our temple at Kirkland, Ohio. In a circular dated June 1, 1833 (History of the Church, Vol. 1, p. 349) it was announced that a house would be built in Kirtland, Ohio and a fund would be started for its construction. It's stated purpose was to have a place where the Elders could gather themselves together in order to prepare themselves to "go forth to the Gentiles for the last time." On that same day the prophet received a revelation which included the measurements of the "house" as being 55 feet by 65 feet. On June 5th (see p. 353) "George A. Smith hauled the first load of stone for the Temple, and Hyrum Smith and Reynolds Cahoon commenced digging the trench for the walls of the Lord's house, and finished the same with their own hands." By July 23, 1833 the cornerstone was laid (H.C. Vol. 1 p. 400)

It took nearly three years from the announcement of the plan to build until the Temple was dedicated on March 27th of 1836. The intervening time between the laying of the cornerstone and said dedication requires 503 pages of the History of the Church to describe what was going on. The prophet was a very busy man. Amidst the many other things going on Joseph did not wait for the dedication of the temple in order to begin to use it for its intended purpose. In order that missionaries might go forth properly prepared to do the Lord's work they needed an endowment. That endowment included gospel instruction, washing and anointing, and awe inspiring spiritual manifestations.

Nearly three months before the dedication and after many successful meetings for the purpose of properly endowing the brethren, Joseph called them together on Saturday, January 6th, 1836. HC, Vol. 2. pp. 391-392, "Called the anointed together to receive the seal of all their blessings. The High Priests and Elders in the council room as usual, the Seventy with the Twelve in the second room, and the Bishops in the third. I labored with each of these quorums for some time to bring them to the order which God had shown to me, which is as follows: The first part to be spent in solemn prayer before God, without any talking or confusion; and the conclusion with a sealing prayer by President

Rigdon, when all quorums were to shout with one accord a solemn hosanna to God and the Lamb, with an Amen, Amen, and Amen; and then all to take seats and lift up their hearts in silent prayer to God, and if any obtain a prophecy or vision, to rise and speak that all may be edified and rejoice together."

"I had considerable trouble to get all the quorums united in this order. I went from room to room repeatedly, and charged each separately, assuring them that it was according to the mind of God, yet, notwithstanding all my labor, while I was in the east room with the Bishops' quorum, I felt, by the spirit, that something was wrong in the quorum of Elders in the west room, and I immediately requested Presidents Oliver Cowdery and Hyrum Smith to go in and see what was the matter, the quorum of Elders had not observed the order which I had given them .... Some of them replied that they had a teacher of their own, and did not wish to be troubled by others. This caused the Spirit of the Lord to withdraw; this interrupted the meeting, and this quorum lost their blessing in a great measure." Joseph went on to recount many grand manifestations of the spirit enjoyed by the other quorums.

The saints gathered on March 27th, 1836 for the dedication (H.C. Vol. 2 pp. 410 - 428). The dedication lasted from 9:00 A.M. until a little after 4:00 P.M.. The doors of the Temple were scheduled to open at 8:00 A.M., but 500-600 saints were already at the doors by 7:00 A.M.. Many had to be turned away and were encouraged to have a meeting in the nearby schoolhouse. Since they were lacking the advantages of modern technology which would have allowed those in the schoolhouse to hear the dedication it was repeated on Thursday, March 31st. Near the end of the original dedication Frederick G. Williams and David Whitmer testified to seeing angels in attendance. Late in the afternoon (H.C. Vol. 2 p. 428), "President Brigham Young gave a short address in tongues, and David W. Patten interpreted, and gave a short exhortation in tongues himself, after which I blessed the congregation in the name of the Lord, and the assembly dispersed a little after four o'clock, having manifested the most quiet demeanor during the whole exercise."

In the evening, after the original dedication, the priesthood brethren returned for a meeting of instruction on the ordinance of washing of feet and on the spirit of prophecy. At the end of the instructional period

Joseph invited the congregation to speak and not to fear to prophesy good concerning the Saints (p. 428). "Brother George A. Smith arose and began to prophesy, when a noise was heard like the sound of a rushing mighty wind, which filled the Temple, and all the congregation simultaneously arose, being moved upon by an invisible power; many began to speak in tongues and prophesy; others saw glorious visions; and I beheld the Temple was filled with angels, which fact I declared to the congregation. The people of the neighborhood came running together (hearing an unusual sound within, and seeing a bright light like a pillar of fire resting upon the Temple), and were astonished at what was taking place. This continued until the meeting closed at eleven P.M." There were 416 members of the priesthood quorums in attendance for this amazing display of the spirit.

Providing for the needs of the poor was a high priority and an early effort in the Church. Traveling in late January of 1831, the prophet, his wife Emma, Sidney Rigdon, and Edward Partridge arrived in Kirtland, Ohio about the first of February (H.C. Vol. 1, p. 146). "The branch of the Church in this part of the Lord's vineyard, which had increased to nearly one hundred members, were striving to do the will of God, so far as they knew it, though some strange notions and false spirits had crept in among them. With a little caution and some wisdom, I soon assisted the brethren and sisters to overcome them. The plan of "common stock," which had existed in what was called 'the family', whose members generally had embraced the everlasting Gospel, was readily abandoned for the more perfect law of the Lord; and the false spirits were easily discerned and rejected by the light of revelation."

According to the History of the Church, "the family" had been living communally before they were proselyted by Elders Oliver Cowdery and Parley P. Pratt said "family" had been members of Sidney Rigdon's church before he was converted (H.C. Vol. 1, p. 124).With regard to the strange notions and false spirits reported by Joseph, B. H. Roberts in the *Comprehensive History of the Church*, Vol. 1, p. 243 has this to say, "It appears that following the proclamation of the Gospel in Kirtland and vicinity, attended as it was by the declaration that the spiritual gifts of that gospel were to be enjoyed, as among the primitive Christians, led to some extravagances of religious frenzy and disorderly conduct;

and while there went out exaggerated and highly colored reports of this exhibition of wild enthusiasm, yet there was enough of fact to bring reproach upon the church. The prophet at once reproved this tendency to over zeal, and immediately corrected the abuses that arose under it." Roberts footnotes at the same site, a non-Mormon author who claims that Joseph inquired of the Lord and was told that the wild enthusiasm was of the Devil.

"The more perfect law of the Lord" which was mentioned in an earlier quotation was referring to the Law of Consecration and is found in D&C 42:30-35;

> "30) And behold, thou wilt remember the poor, and consecrate of thy properties for their support that which thou hast to impart unto them, with a covenant and a deed which cannot be broken.
> 31) And inasmuch as ye impart of your substance unto the poor, ye will do it unto me; and they shall be laid before the bishop of my church and his counselors, two of the elders, or high priests, such as he shall appoint or has appointed and set apart for that purpose.
> 32) And it shall come to pass, that after they are laid before the bishop of my church, and after that he has received these testimonies concerning the consecration of the properties of my church, that they cannot be taken from the church, agreeable to my commandments, every man shall be made accountable unto me, a steward over his own property, or that which he has received by consecration, as much as is sufficient for himself and family.
> 33) And again, if there shall be properties in the hands of the Church or any Individuals of it, more than is necessary for their support after this first consecration, which is a residue to be consecrated unto the bishop, it shall be kept to administer to those who have not, from time to time, that every man who has need may be amply supplied and receive according to his wants.

34) Therefore, the residue shall be kept in my storehouse, to administer to the poor and the needy, as shall be appointed by the high council of the church, and the bishop and his council;

35) And for the purpose of purchasing lands for the public benefit of the church, and building houses of worship, and building up of the New Jerusalem which is hereafter to be revealed –"

The law of consecration is not about communal living, but is more like the parable of the talents in Matthew, chapter 25:14-23;

"14) For the kingdom of heaven is as a man travelling into a far country, who called his own servants, and delivered unto them his goods.

15) And unto one he gave five talents, to another two, and another one; to every man according to his several ability; and straightway took his journey.

16) Then he that had received the five talents went and traded with the same, and made them other five talents.

17) and likewise he that had received two, he also gained other two.

18) But he that had received one went and digged in the earth, and hid his lord's money.

19) After a long time the lord of those servants cometh and reckoneth with them.

20) And so he that had received five talents came and brought other five talents, saying, Lord, thou deliveredst unto me five talents: behold, I have gained beside them five talents more.

21) His lord said unto him, Well done, thou good and faithful servant: thou hast been faithful over a few things, I will make thee ruler over many things: enter thou into the joy of thy lord.

22) He also that had received two talents came and said, Lord, thou deliveredst unto me two talents: behold, I have gained two other talents beside them.

23) His lord said unto him, Well done, good and faithful servant; thou hast been faithful over a few things, I will make thee ruler many things: enter thou into the joy of they lord."

As you read further on you find out that the servant who buried his talent did not fare well.

Though the law of consecration is not communal living, it is about caring for the poor. It is the principle upon which the New Jerusalem was to operate. The saints were not able to remain in Kirtland, Ohio or to establish themselves in Independence, Missouri where the New Jerusalem was to be built. That, along with the Nauvoo period will be covered in later chapters.

CHAPTER 3

MORMON MIRACLES

This chapter on miracles contains just a few examples of the power of God which has been manifest upon the heads of the Latter-Day Saints. The Lord has blest us for our efforts to serve him and cursed us for our follies. He has delivered his priesthood to us by which we call down the blessings of heaven on each other. The blessing of the sick is an ordinance which is performed by those who hold the Melchizedek Priesthood. I have participated in blessings on the sick and injured which, if the doctor's diagnosis was correct, resulted in improvement which would seem to have been miraculous. Those incidents I believe to have been the result of the faith of the person who was injured or sick and I thank the Lord for the privilege of having been able to be part of those incidents though I take no credit for the happy results. I have received some training in foot reflexology for which I have some slight gift by which I have lessened pain and discomfort for a few family members and friends. While I was excommunicated the progress of my physical infirmities did so much damage to my wrists that I rarely perform that service.

CHC, Vol. 1, pp.201-202, often called the first miracle of the church, the case of demonic possession of Newel Knight was quite a spectacle. His limbs were twisted in every shape possible to imagine. Eventually he was caught up off the floor and tossed around the apartment until he finally ended up pressed against the ceiling. When the prophet managed to grasp his hand Knight regained enough of his senses to ask Joseph to cast out the devil which had possession of him. Knight was immediately relieved from the power which had hold of him. He declared having seen the evil spirit leave him and disappear from sight. Joseph gave God the glory. About eight or ten neighbors and relatives had witnessed this unusual scene, most of whom joined the church afterwards. This was in late April of 1830, not many days after the Church was organized.

CHC, Vol. 2, pp. 18-19, "during the summer of 1839, the Saints who had been driven from Missouri had been gathering to Nauvoo. The physical and emotional stress they had endured left them easy prey to the malaria which was common to the area. The Smith home, yard and tent were crowded with weary and ailing escapees from the mobs of Missouri. By the 22nd of July Joseph himself had fallen ill and spent several days sick and overshadowed with sadness for the trials his people were enduring. The spirit of God rested upon him and he immediately was healed and began to administer to the sick in his home and yard. He then went from house to house calling on the sick to arise and be healed. 'They obeyed and were healed.' In the company of several of the leading brethren he crossed the river to Montrose and healed the sick there. It was a day-long manifestation of God's love and power. The most remarkable case involved one Elijah Fordham. "He was almost unconscious and nearly dead. Bending over him, the Prophet asked the dying man if he knew him, and believed him to be a servant of God. In a whisper Fordham replied that he did. Joseph then took him by the hand, 'and with an energy that would have awoke the dead' he commanded him in the name of Jesus Christ to arise from his bed and walk. Brother Fordham leaped from his bed, removed the bandages and mustard plasters from his feet, dressed himself, ate a bowl of bread and milk, and accompanied the brethren to the other houses on their mission of love."

HC Vol. 1, pp.215-216 and taken from Hayden's History of the Disciples (a Campbellite work). pp.250-1. "Ezra Booth, of Mantua, a Methodist preacher of much more than ordinary culture, and with strong natural abilities, in company with his wife, Mr. and Mrs. Johnson, and some other citizens of this place [Hiram], visited Smith at his home in Kirtland, in 1831. Mrs. Johnson had been afflicted for some time with a lame arm, and was not at the time of the visit able to lift her hand to her head. The party visited Smith partly out of curiosity, and partly to see for themselves what there might be in the new doctrine. During the interview the conversation turned on the subject of supernatural gifts, such as were conferred in the days of the Apostles. Someone said, 'Here is Mrs. Johnson with a lame arm: has God given any power to man now on the earth to cure her?' A few moments later, when the conversation had turned in another direction, Smith rose, and walking across the room, taking Mrs. Johnson by the hand, said in the most solemn and impressive manner: 'Woman, in the name of the Lord Jesus Christ I command thee to be whole,' and immediately left the room. The company were awe-stricken at the infinite presumption of the man, and the calm assurance with which he spoke. The sudden mental and moral shock–I know not how better to explain the well-attested fact–electrified the rheumatic arm–Mrs. Johnson at once lifted it up with ease, and on her return home the next day she was able to do her washing without difficulty or pain."

HC Vol. 2, pp.103-105, June 19th, 1834; Starting out on May 5th, 1834 (p.63) Joseph and a group of men were on their way from Kirtland to Missouri with "horses, wagons, and firearms, and all sorts of munitions of war of the most portable kind for self defense". They were going to help their brethren in Missouri who had been robbed and plundered of nearly all their effects. They had many adventures, but one account stood out for me. With many mishaps to hinder them they ended up on the evening of June 19th camped on an elevated piece of land between Little Fishing and Big Fishing rivers; "As we halted and were making preparations for the night, five men armed with guns rode into our camp, and told us we should 'see hell before morning;' and their accompanying oaths partook of all the malice of demons. They told us that sixty men were coming from Richmond, Ray County, and seventy more from Clay county to join the Jackson county mob, who had sworn our utter destruction."

"During this day, the Jackson county mob to the number of about two hundred made arrangements to cross the Missouri river above the mouth of Fishing river at Williams' ferry into Clay county and be ready to meet the Richmond mob near Fishing river ford for our utter destruction; but after the first scow load of about forty had been set over the river, the scow in returning was met by a squall and had great difficulty in reaching the Jackson side by dark."

"When these five men were in our camp, swearing vengeance, the wind, thunder, and rising cloud indicated an approaching storm, and in a short time after they left the rain and hail began to fall. The storm was tremendous; wind and rain, hail and thunder met them in great wrath, and soon softened their direful courage, and frustrated all their designs to 'kill Joe Smith and his army.' Instead of continuing a cannonading which they commenced when the sun was about one hour high, they crawled under wagons, into hollow trees, and filled one old shanty, til the storm was over when their ammunition was soaked, and the forty in Clay county were extremely anxious in the morning to return to Jackson having experienced the pitiless pelting of the storm all night; and as soon as arrangements could be made, this 'forlorn hope' took the 'back track' for Independence to join the main body of the mob, fully satisfied, as were those survivors of the company who were drowned that when Jehovah fights they would rather be absent. The gratification is too terrible. Very little hail fell in our camp, but from half a mile to a mile around, the stones or lumps of ice cut down the crops of corn and vegetation generally, even cutting limbs from trees, while the trees, themselves were twisted into withes by the wind. The lightning flashed incessantly which caused it to be so light in our camp through the night that we could discern the most minute objects; and the roaring of the thunder was tremendous. The earth trembled and quaked, the rain fell in torrents, and united it seemed as if the mandate of vengeance had gone forth from the God of battles to protect His servants from the destruction of their enemies, for the hail fell on them and not on us, and we suffered no harm except the blowing down of some of our tents and getting wet; while our enemies had holes made in their hats and otherwise received damage even the breaking of their rifle stocks and the fleeing of their horses through fear and pain."

"Many of my little band sheltered in an old meeting house through this night and in the morning the water in Big Fishing river was about forty feet deep where the previous evening, it was no more than to our ankles and our enemies swore that the water rose thirty feet in thirty minutes in the Little Fishing river. They reported that one of their men was killed by lighting and that another had his hand torn off by his horse drawing his hand between the logs of a corn crib while he was holding him on the inside. They declared that if that was the way God fought for the Mormons, they might as well go about their business."

The seagulls and the crickets: When Brigham Young led the Saints westward, he sent a scouting party ahead. Orson Pratt was part of that party. At a discourse in the Bowery in Great Salt Lake City he described his first view of the Salt Lake Valley. JD, Vol. 12, p.88 he said; "What did I see when I came into this valley? I saw some few green bushes on yonder bench, but saw but little life throughout the valley, except a certain insect that was afterwards called a cricket. I saw them cropping the few isolated bushes, and gnawing everything green around them. The land on yonder bench was all parched up, and the soil as we went down still further, also dry and baked; but as we neared the waters we could see there was a little moisture round the banks. It was really a solitary place"

We will continue the account as told by Orson Hyde on Sept 24, 1853, JD Vol. 2, p.114; "Behold when they arrived here, all they had to subsist upon, until they raised it from the soil, was in their wagons. There were no crops to come to; there was nothing provided to cheer them at the end of their long and toilsome journey; and the skeletons of cattle might be seen walking to and fro, without anything provided to feed them through a long winter. And then, when they had plowed up the soil, and sowed seed in the earth, and the fields began to show an evidence of a future supply, the crickets came in millions from the mountains, and nearly devoured all that grew; everything that germinated in the shape of food for man was eaten by the insects. But before they had completed the work of destruction, the hand of providence prepared agents, and sent them to destroy the destroyer; a circumstance that was rare, one that was never known to exist before, and never since to any extent—behold, the gulls came in swarms, and as clouds, and eat up the crickets, and checked them in their destructive career; and there was just enough saved to feed the hungry with a scanty morsel.'"

"There are many before me this morning who can no doubt remember well when their meal bags were perfectly empty, with only a distant prospect of their being replenished; and when a cow was slaughtered, rare as it was, they eat everything; even the hide was boiled, dressed, and eaten, and everything else, external and internal, that possibly could be eaten was eaten; there was nothing lost. One man said to me, 'I labored hard under the pangs of hunger to put up a little adobie cabin and prepare to live, and at the same time my wife and children, pale and want, were ranging the hills and benches to find thistles and roots to eat, which we boiled in the milk of the remaining cows the wolves had not eaten.'"

On February 10, 1856 Orson Pratt told the Saints why they were afflicted with plagues of insects and droughts. JD Vol. 3, pp296-297; "You have a foundation laid, and if you will rightly build upon it, it will far outreach the present civilization of the world, and I have no doubt but that you will build upon it. ... The Latter-Day Saints have their foundation right, and when they take hold and rear the superstructure, it will be one of the greatest ever constructed by the inhabitants of this earth. I do not despair when I see such a foundation, for if we are not now altogether what we should be, I believe that the Lord will whip us into it; I have no doubt of that."

"... I am as convinced that the Lord will whip us into this diligent course, as I am that I am standing before you. Why? Because this is the kingdom, this is the people and the Church of the living God, and just as surely as He is our God, will He purify this people by famine, by war, by sickness, by death, by various judgments, and by the flame of devouring fire. We cannot escape the course of purification. What is more visible to the eye than the dealings of God, our Father, with us for the past year? First came the innumerable swarms of insects by the millions, sweeping of our crops, then the drought drying them up as does the sun the dew, consuming nearly all the insects had left. How was this? Because the snows were kept from the mountains during the previous winter. What next? The drought continued month after month, preventing the grass from growing as it has done in falls of previous years, and thus leaving our ground destitute of feed. Then what? A severe winter, deep snow, so deep as to cover the few spears of grass that were left. Thus one calamity after another, one punishment after another is enough to convince us that all proceeded from the hand of the Lord our God. Has He not a purpose in this? Is it not an affliction to us, to you and to me? Do you not feel it? Will it not learn us a lesson? Yes, it will."

"I feel to say in my heart, O Lord, chasten me, let thy chastening hand be upon me, if thou seest there is no other way of escape. I would much rather be chastened than to heap up an abundance of this world's goods, and neglect some of he most important duties of my religion. Hence, when I pray in relation to myself, my prayer is for the Lord to chasten me, and also in relation to this people my prayer is, O lord, let thy chastening hand be upon this people, until they learn to obey those good and wholesome counsels that are poured out from this stand by those who preside over us."

CHAPTER 4

MORMON BACKSLIDING

Before the Book of Mormon was fully translated, Joseph tested the Lord's patience and lost his gift for a time. The details (HC Vol. 1:21) involve one Martin Harris who was serving as Joseph's scribe in translating the gold plates and who desired to take 116 pages of the manuscript home to show to a few persons. This was about the middle of June, 1828. Martin was unable to talk the prophet into allowing it, but insisted that Joseph ask the Lord through the Urim and Thummim. The answer was "no" the first and second times, but Martin insisted that Joseph ask a third time whereupon permission was given. Martin had strict limitations as to whom the manuscript was to be shown, but he carelessly displayed them far and wide until they were stolen. The Lord was very displeased that Joseph had troubled him so many times only to have the manuscript stolen. The consequence was that the Lord took the Urim and Thummim away from Joseph for a time. While waiting for Martin Harris to return the manuscript Joseph's wife, Emma, delivered a son who died shortly thereafter with Emma's life still hanging in the balance (CHC Vol. 1, p.110).

Some time in July, the Lord returned the Urim and Thummim to Joseph long enough for him to receive a revelation which is recorded as Section 3 of the D&C. Selected verses follow;

6) And behold, how oft you have transgressed the commandments and the laws of God, and have gone on in the persuasions of men.
7) For, behold, you should not have feared man more than God. Although men set at naught the counsels of God, and despise his words-
8) Yet you should have been faithful and he would have extended his arm and supported you against all the fiery darts of the adversary: and he would have been with you in every time of trouble."

Does verse eight suggest merely that God left Joseph comfortless when his newborn son died and while Emma was near death, or does it mean that Joseph's son would not have died had Joseph not disappointed God?

The work suffered a serious setback a few years later during the nationwide economic bust of 1835-1837. Joseph had been attempting to establish a bank just prior to the bust. Government officials would not allow it, but an enterprise was formed called the Kirtland Safety Society which sold shares. As Joseph had been instrumental in organizing it the failure of the Society created many enemies for him and a mob of apostates among the leaders of the Church. According to Readings in LDS Church History, Vol.1, p.239, "There were in it no less than four members of the Twelve Apostles, several of the 'witnesses of the Book of Mormon,' and many influential elders."

The anger of the mob reached such heights that Joseph and Sidney Rigdon fled Kirtland on the 12th of January, 1838 at ten o'clock in the evening. H.C. Vol. 4, p.166; "It would be gratifying to my mind to see the Saints in Kirtland flourish, but think the time is not yet come; and I assure you it never will until a different order of things be established and a different spirit manifested. ... It is in consequence of aspiring men that Kirtland has been forsaken. How frequently has your humble servant been envied in his office by such characters who endeavored to raise themselves to power at his expense, and seeing it impossible to do so, resorted to foul slander and abuse, and other means to effect his overthrow."

One example of the many efforts to oppose Joseph which could be made involves that same Martin Harris who lost the first 116 pages of the Book of Mormon manuscript. H.C. Vol. 2, p. 26, January, 1834; "The council proceeded to investigate certain charges presented by Elder Rigdon against Martin Harris; one was that he told A. C. Russell, Esq., that Joseph drank too much liquor when he was translating the Book of Mormon; and that he wrestled with many men and threw them; and that he (Harris) exalted himself above Joseph, in that he said, 'Brother Joseph knew not the contents of the Book of Mormon, until it was translated, but that he himself knew all about it before it was translated.'"

Even as the Saints were establishing themselves in Kirtland, Joseph was attempting to establish a foothold in Missouri in order to build up the prophesied Center Place, the New Jerusalem, near Independence, Missouri. That effort was likewise failing. Reading in the Book of Mormon in Ether 13:6&8;

> "6) And that a New Jerusalem should be built upon this land, unto the remnant of the seed of Joseph [the Biblical Joseph], for which things there has been a type.
> 8) Wherefore, the remnant of the house of Joseph shall be built upon this land; and it shall be a land of their inheritance; and they shall build up a holy city unto the Lord, like unto the Jerusalem of old; and they shall no more be confounded, until the end come when the earth shall pass away."

From the above quotation it does not appear that the Gentiles were meant to establish the New Jerusalem. That honor was to be left to the tribe of Joseph. It appears to me that the Lord gave Joseph Smith, with the help of the Gentiles he had gathered, the chance to make the attempt knowing that there were not enough worthy saints at his disposal to succeed. It doesn't sound to me like the Lord had promised Joseph Smith a sure thing. D&C 58:6-7, August 1st, 1831;

6) Behold, verily I say unto you, for this cause I have sent you-that you might be obedient, and that your hearts might be prepared to bear testimony of the things which are to come;

7) and also that you might be honored in laying the foundation, and in bearing record of the land upon which the Zion of God shall stand."

In late September of 1832 they were given a more positive hope of the nearness of the glory to come. D&C 84:4-5;

4) Verily this is the word of the Lord, that the city of New Jerusalem shall be built by the gathering of the saints, beginning at this place, even the place of the temple, which temple shall be reared in this generation.

5) For verily this generation shall not all pass away until an house shall be built unto the Lord, and a cloud shall rest upon it, which cloud shall be even the glory of the Lord, which shall fill the house."

On the 16th of August, 1834 Joseph wrote a letter to the High Council of Zion setting the time of the redemption of Zion and the price of failure. H.C. Vol. 2, p.145; "...use every effort to ... be in readiness to move into Jackson County in two years from the eleventh of September next, which is the appointed time for the redemption of Zion. If –verily I say into you–if the Church with one united effort perform their duties; if they do this, the work shall be complete–if they do not this in all humility, making preparation from this forth, ... and if we do not exert ourselves to the utmost in gathering up the strength of the Lord's house that this thing may be accomplished, behold there remaineth a scourge for the Church, even that they shall be driven from city to city..."

H.C. Vol. 1, p. 136, in a letter dated Jan. 14, 1833, to William W. Phelps who was one of the brethren in Zion Joseph wrote; "... we have the satisfaction of knowing that the Lord approves of us, and has accepted us and established His name in Kirtland for the salvation of the nations; for the Lord will have a place whence His word will go forth, in these last days, in purity; for if Zion will not purify herself, so as to be approved of in all things, in His sight, He will seek another people;"

H.C. Vol. 1, p. 320-321, in a letter written that same day by a Conference of Twelve High Priests in a conference at Kirtland the brethren in Zion were further admonished; "Zion is the place where the temple will be built, and the people gathered, but all people upon that holy land being under condemnation, the Lord will cut off, if they repent not, and bring another race upon it, that will serve Him. The Lord will seek another place to bring forth and prepare his word to go forth to the nations, and as we said before, so we say again. Brother Joseph will not settle in Zion, except he repent, and serve God, and obey the new covenant. With this explanation, the conference sanctions Brother Joseph's letter."

After the effort to establish themselves in Zion had failed, Joseph made a prophesy on August 6th, 1844; "I prophesied that the Saints would be driven to the Rocky Mountains, many would apostatize, other would be put death by our persecutors or lose their lives in consequence of exposure or disease, and some of you will live to go and assist in making settlements and build cities and see the Saints become a mighty people in the midst of the Rocky Mountains." In the chapter on Nauvoo we will see how the Saints being driven to the Great Salt Lake Valley fulfilled a curse delivered by Jeremiah in the Old Testament.

There is no doubt that the saints were being tested. The Book of Mormon promises that the great amount of information, the greater things from plates which Joseph was not allowed to translate would eventually be revealed for translation after we have proved that we believe the lesser things already given us. In September of 1832 Joseph received a revelation in which we find a reference as to how they were doing in D&C 84;

> 54) And your minds in times past have been darkened because of unbelief, and because you have treated lightly the things you have received.
> 55) Which vanity and unbelief have brought the whole church under condemnation.

56) And this condemnation resteth upon the children of Zion, even all.

57) And they shall remain under this condemnation until they remember the new covenant, even the Book of Mormon and the former commandments which I have written-"

So how did the Saints do in believing the lesser things; In Alma 33:16, "For behold, thou art angry O Lord, with this people because they will not understand thy mercies which thou hast bestowed upon them because of thy Son.", was spoken against the Children of Israel by a prophet in the Northern Kingdom. For me this is closely connected to a fundamental belief stated numerous times in the Bible, the Book of Mormon, and the Doctrine and Covenants and that belief is the equality of believers. Whenever there is a discussion on the subject of blacks of African descent being denied the priesthood up until the announcement in 1978, some will admit to being surprised by the announcement and some will not.

To my shame I must admit to being surprised when the announcement of the availability of the priesthood to men of all races finally came in 1978. I am not the first to finally believe that the matter of the equality of the believers was a test which the Latter-Day Saints failed, but it took some years for me to come to that conclusion. Somehow I had overlooked the many passages demanding the equality of believers. I even missed those verses in D&C 38: 24-27 wherein the Lord makes it clear that He is like a man with 12 sons who serve him obediently. He cannot claim to be just if he says to one of them, "Be thou clothed in robes and sit thou here; and to the other; be thou clothed in rags and sit thou there". At the beginning of this passage He told them twice to "let every man esteem his brother as himself".

A few years later when the garments of the Holy Priesthood were made available to the Melchizedek priesthood and their spouses in Nauvoo at least one black man, Elijah Abel had been ordained by Joseph Smith, but I don't believe he was allowed to receive temple clothing. In the December essay on Race and the Priesthood a positive spin was placed on the account by mentioning that Elijah Abel had attended temple ceremonies in the Kirtland Temple and was baptized as proxy for deceased relatives without mentioning that he was not allowed to participate in ceremonies requiring temple clothing. Too many of the saints brought their racism with them when they became members of the Church and they took delight in passages in the Pearl of Great Price which they thought gave them precedent for withholding the priesthood from blacks. Certainly the withholding of the temple clothing from blacks who held the priesthood leaves no need for clearer evidence to show that racists among the Saints did not intend to esteem their black brothers and sisters as equal to themselves.

When Brigham Young became the leader of the LDS Church he made it clear that he never wanted or expected to see the time when blacks were considered equal. More about that later. How he must have resented Joseph for ordaining Elijah Abel. For a long time I thought that the general authorities of the church were unanimous in that belief. I was aware of one black man ordained by Joseph Smith. Joseph ordained Elijah Abel in 1836. He was eventually ordained a Seventy and served more than one mission according to Darius Gray.

In a later chapter I will cover the loss of our prophet before the Saints were driven out of Nauvoo. Once the Saints had lost their prophet, Joseph Smith, Brigham Young as the president of the Quorum of Twelve Apostles was transformed before their eyes in a conference. He took on the appearance of Joseph Smith which convinced the Saints that he was their new leader and they followed him to Utah. With Brigham Young as their prophet; when it comes to believing the Book of Mormon, how well did Latter-Day Saints measure up when they settled in the west?

When Isaiah is speaking prophetically of the Savior in Isaiah 53:10, "He shall see his seed", who is his seed? Whereas there are many Biblical references to Christians becoming the seed of Abraham by adoption and becoming joint heirs with Christ, the Book of Mormon says it very plainly in Mosiah 15:10-13,

> 10) "And now I say unto you, who shall declare his generation? Behold, I say unto you, that when his soul has been made an offering for sin he shall see his seed. And now what say ye? And who shall be his seed?

11) Behold I say unto you, that whosoever has heard the words of the prophets, yea, all the holy prophets who have prophesied concerning the coming of the Lord – I say unto you, that all those who have hearkened unto their words, and believed that the Lord would redeem his people, and have looked forward to that day for a remission of their sins, I say unto you, that these are his seed, or they are the heirs of the Kingdom of God.
12) For these are they whose sins he has borne; these are they for whom he has died, to redeem from their transgressions. And now, are they not his seed?
13) Yea, and are not the prophets, every one that has opened his mouth to prophesy, that has not fallen into transgression, I mean all the holy prophets ever since the world began? I say unto you that they are his seed."

You will find in vol.2, p. 82 of the *Journal of Discourses* that on October 6, 1854 the brethren in Salt Lake City had a different idea. Orson Hyde, said, speaking in conference on the subject of The Marriage Relations, "We say it was Jesus Christ who was married to be brought into the relation whereby he could see his seed, before he was crucified. 'Has he indeed passed by the nature of angels and taken upon himself the seed of Abraham, to die without leaving a seed to bear his name on the earth?" No. But when the secret is fully out, the seed of the blessed shall be gathered in, in the last days; and he who has not the blood of Abraham flowing in his veins, who has not one particle of the Savior's in him, I am afraid is a stereotyped Gentile, who will be left out and not be gathered in the last days; for I tell you it is the chosen of God, the seed of the blessed that shall be gathered."

Elder Hyde went on to speculate as to how many wives the Savior had. Following brother Hyde's talk, Brigham said a few words starting with this opening paragraph, "I do not wish to eradicate any items from the lecture Elder Hyde has given us this evening, but simply to give you my views, in a few words, on the portion touching Bishops and Deacons."

We no longer believe the above and many other strange beliefs promoted by Brigham Young and I dare say that few members are even aware that He taught such things. But the belief that blacks should not hold the priesthood was carried with the Saints to Utah with additional racist dogma added to the growing accumulation of strange doctrine developing there.

When I joined the Church shortly after graduating from high school, the attitude of Mormons towards blacks was of interest to me. I discovered additional scriptures to study and a huge amount of commentaries to guide me in becoming familiar with my new faith. The commentaries I studied rejected that blatant racism which promoted notions of an innate inferiority of blacks and the black skin being a curse, but they did quote past leaders of the Church who insisted that blacks would never receive the priesthood in mortality. Thanks to Darius Gray, a black Latter-Day Saint of great faith and burning testimony, I have since become aware of at least one of our prophets, David O. McKay, who did not agree that they would never obtain the priesthood in mortality. There is an obvious conclusion to be drawn, as the Apostle Paul declared in I Cor.11:19, "For there must also be heresies among you that they which are approved may be made manifest among you." Elder Bruce R. McConkie referred to this as part of the sifting process of the Church.

When we see negative things said about the children of Israel in the scriptures I marvel that we imagine we have to look outside the Church for modern examples of the same. Alma 33:16, "For behold, he said: Thou art angry, O Lord, with this people because they will not understand thy mercies which thou has bestowed upon them because of thy Son."

Something which I found in my own studies long ago from the History of the Church, vol. 3, page 296-297, an excerpt from a letter written while Joseph was in Liberty Jail and completed on March 25, 1839. Joseph described how the activities of renegade members of the church and outside persecutors related to it, but I maintain that it should be obvious to all that it is a general principle. "But I beg leave to say unto you, brethren, that ignorance, superstition and bigotry placing itself where it ought not, is oftentimes in the way of the prosperity of this Church; like the torrent of rain from the mountains, that floods the most pure and crystal stream with mire, and dirt, and filthiness, and obscures everything that was clear before, and all rushes along in one general deluge; but time weathers tide: and notwithstanding we are rolled in the mire of the flood for the time being, the next surge peradventure, as time rolls on, may bring to us the fountain as clear as crystal, and as pure as snow; while the filthiness, flood wood and rubbish is left and purged out by the way."

I would not have returned to the Church if I was not convinced that the promise to the quorum of twelve in D&C 112:13 still holds true. "And after their temptations, and much tribulations, behold, I, the Lord, will feel after them, and if they harden not their hearts, and stiffen not their necks against me, they shall be converted and I will heal them." It seems evident to me that said promise still holds true for each of us today. I don't imagine we will come to the fountain clear as crystal and pure as snow until the Lord is ready to separate the wheat from the tares. Like many members of the Church I didn't realize on what shaky ground the practice of withholding the priesthood from African blacks was established.

When the announcement that the priesthood would be available to men of all races came forth in 1978, it was obviously out of tune with the things spoken by some of our past leaders, but not out-of-tune with our scriptures. Brigham Young had not only loudly proclaimed that blacks would never receive the priesthood in morality, JD, Vol. 11, p. 272, but he went so far as to say at an earlier date (J.D. Vol. 7, p.290-291) that the seed of Cain would not receive the priesthood until all the other descendants of Adam had received the priesthood. Additionally he said that the penalty for a white man of the chosen seed to mix his seed with the seed of Cain was death, and always would be, JD, Vol. 10, p.110 . Call it an unwillingness to be judgmental, false pride, or concern for the feelings of the general membership of the Church, the brethren were unwilling to mention any former disagreement among the previous leaders of the Church. The letter from the First Presidency announcing the change in policy says, "Aware of the promises made by the prophets and presidents of the Church who have preceded us that at some time, in God's eternal plan, all of our brethren who are worthy may receive the priesthood ...". The Letter dated June 8, 1978 carefully allows us to believe that previously only unanimity existed on the idea that the black's time would come in mortality. Some may admire that kind of spin, but I call it sophistry when they make it so easy to jump to false conclusions.

How should we look upon the misleading nature of the letter proclaiming the availability of the priesthood to men of all races? I'm willing to look at it as being the result of an unwillingness to be judgmental of the brethren who faced mobs wanting to commit genocide. I suspect that the brethren mercifully gave the diehard racists a little wiggle room so that they would not feel they were being chased out of the Church. But, the Church Education system and many of the brethren generally appear to have taken the refusal to be candid as a signal that cover-up is the name of the game we are playing. Oh, they are willing to admit that it is possible for a prophet to make a mistake, especially if it is on an irrelevant topic such as Joseph Fielding Smith's proclamation that man would never reach the moon. But, they don't like to see undeniable evidence placed before the members of false doctrine.

There remains for me the fear of something sinister which may be going on with regard to the cover-up of lack of unity which existed on the topic of the blacks and the priesthood. I recall some of the speculation surrounding the change in policy. Some diehard racists were saying that the general authorities were simply giving in to political pressure. Did our leaders wish to leave diehard racists the option of believing that African Blacks should not have the priesthood, but we would have to allow them to hold the priesthood because of pressure from the civil rights movement. Thinking that the change in policy was made only because of outside pressure is dangerous because it gives false hope to those in the Church and outside the Church who would like to promote other changes in the Church.

What we have in the Church now is too much pablum. Pablum was a cereal for infants which I insisted on eating until I was five years old. In the Spring Conference of 2012 one of our leaders recounted Brigham Young telling the Saints how the Federal Troops would be driven back in his talk in the morning session. Then, in the afternoon session Brigham said something like, "This morning I gave you my ideas on what we would do about the Federal Troops. Now I'm going to give you the Lord's will". I will be pleasantly surprised when our leaders come clean and tell us how much of that which Brigham Young taught was utter nonsense and perhaps utter nonsense was what the Saints rated from the Lord. Perhaps Brigham Young was one of the scourges the saints were to be punished by or tested by. Surely the Lord had purpose in allowing Brigham Young to lead the Church for so many years.

In the mid 1970s, I had spoken out against the racist dogma which accompanied the then current practice of refusing to allow blacks of African descent to hold the priesthood. To my dismay some were trying to make the Church a haven for racists as they invited racists to come into the Church because "We know how to keep the blacks in their place." I also spoke out against the secret practice of polygamy by members of the church in California. I was surprised by the lack of willingness from my Stake President to respond to my complaints about things done to me and I was concerned about the popularity of some of the doctrine being promoted, more about that later. My concerns led me to reevaluate the negative information presented me by my Southern Baptist minister when I told him I was thinking about joining the LDS Church. My Mormon friends and the books they steered me to seem to answer the accusations against Brigham Young and Joseph Smith at the time, but that which was being promoted by church members where I lived in the 1970s made a closer study seem to be important.

My initial study of the accusations about Brigham Young's teachings had taken me to suggestions that Brigham had been taken out of context or misquoted as Joseph Fielding Smith does on page 96 of the first volume of *Doctrines of Salvation*. My in- depth study later showed me that those commentaries written by General Authorities of the church were mistaken about Brigham's teachings. I had been misinformed by my LDS friends who had fallen for the efforts of those who should have known better than to try to sweep negative things under the carpet. Finding out that our history was being covered up led me to think that the Lord had cast off the Mormons and I left the Church. Twenty five years later some dreams led me to conclude that I had been mistaken. After all, why would the Lord cast of the Mormons after only a few decades when He had stuck by the Children of Israel for hundreds of years.

Before you read any further, I want you to know that the LDS Church is full of some of the finest people on the planet. Many active

Mormons, though not all of them, are well studied students of the scriptures, have strong testimonies of the Gospel and are what I would class as the "salt of the earth". I thought it was polygamists and racists who had been trying to make me feel unwelcome in the church back then, but I have come to realize that there is a third group of pious snobs I have to face. The "All is well in Zion" crowd believes that anything done by or said by our leaders is perfectly alright just because they did it or said it and to suggest otherwise can get you in trouble with them. I will repeat what I said earlier, "I know for a fact that the current First Presidency of the church is above that kind of snobbery. About a year after my rebaptism I appealed to them in a letter to restore my blessings. In the letter I told President Monson that my testimony does not require me to believe that all of our leaders have been true to their callings, nor does it require me to consider the Pearl of Great Price to be completely credible. President Monson sent Elder Kenneth Johnson of the Seventy to restore my blessings which included my priesthood."

When our leaders put an end to open racism in the church with the announcement that the priesthood was available to men of all races I was already too close to leaving the Church. The announcement came with such unanimity that Elder Bruce R. McConkie announced that everyone was to forget everything he had written or stated on the subject of blacks and the priesthood. In the October conference of 1980 Elder Mark E. Petersen declared the arguments supporting the Adam-God theory to be false without calling them the Adam/God theory. Although he made reference in his closing remarks to false teachers and advocators of false doctrine who come among us he did not mention that the doctrine he attacked was Brigham Young's. It is my contention that some people with personal agendas to advance doctrine not in keeping with the gospel of Jesus Christ have infiltrated the Church of Jesus Christ of Latter-Day Saints.

I have gone through the twenty six volume *Journal of Discourses* and read all of Brigham Young's speeches and taken notes on many of them. I tell you in all soberness that the things taught by Brigham Young are better explained by a verse in the Book of Mormon, namely Jacob 4:14. It reads, "But behold, the Jews were a stiff necked people; and they despised the words of plainness, ... and sought for things that they could not understand. Wherefore, because of their blindness, which blindness came by looking beyond the mark, ... God hath ... delivered unto them many things which they cannot understand, because they desired it. And because they desired it God hath done it, that they may stumble."

This may sound a bit harsh when directed at some of our past leaders, but the Saints did not end up in the Great Salt Lake Valley instead of their promised center place in Independence, Mo. because their behavior had been above reproach. The outlandish things they taught in contradiction to the scriptures was not simply a case of difference of opinions.

The saints were tested, not only in what they believed, but also in what they might ask for. D&C 88:64-65,

> 64) Whatsoever ye shall ask the Father in my name it shall be given unto you, that is expedient for you;
> 65) And if ye ask anything that is not expedient for you, it shall turn unto your condemnation."

As Latter-Day Saints we are proud of our "Word of Wisdom" given in Section 89 of our Doctrine and Covenants. A much more general and shorter version was given in D&C 59:16-23.

> 16) Verily I say, that inasmuch as ye do this, the fullness of the earth is yours, the beasts of the field and the fowls of the air, and that which climbeth upon the trees and walketh upon the earth;
> 17) Yea, and the herb, and the good things which come of the earth, whether for food or for raiment, or for houses, or for barns, or for orchards, or for gardens, or for vineyards;
> 18) Yea, all things which come of the earth, in the season thereof, are made for the benefit and the use of man, both to please the eye and to gladden the heart;
> 19) Yea, for food and for raiment, for taste and for smell, to strengthen the body and to enliven the soul.
> 20) And it pleaseth God that he hath given all these things unto man; for unto this end were they made to be used, with judgment, not to excess, neither by extortion.

21) And in nothing doth man offend God, or against none is his wrath kindled, save those who confess not his hand in all things, and obey not his commandments.
22) Behold, this is according to the law and the prophets; wherefore, trouble me no more concerning this matter.
23) But learn that he who doeth the works of righteousness shall receive his reward, even peace in this world, and eternal life in the world to come."

Notice that verse 22 gives a stern warning, "trouble me no more concerning this matter." Notice also that verse 20 states that the things thus listed were "made to be used, with judgment, not to excess, neither by extortion." While the Saints were thus advised they were free to use their judgment in accordance with D&C 58:26, "For behold, it is not meet that I should command in all things; for he that is compelled in all things, the same is a slothful and not a wise servant; wherefore he receiveth no reward." The key here is that he that is compelled in all things doesn't get to show his wisdom.

The Lord had good reason to avoid being specific on matters of the "dos and don'ts" of nutrition. We are all different in our nutritional needs and ability to tolerate different foods. I have found the blood type diet very useful in regaining my health. I take verse 26 as an invitation to study alternative and traditional medicine and experiment in order to find what is most effective for me. Those who enjoy perfect health will not be motivated to follow my example.

But Joseph did trouble the Lord further. He tired of Emma's complaints about the mess left by those who used tobacco at the many meetings Joseph held and which she cleaned up after. The result was section 89 which we call the "Word of Wisdom".

The "Word of Wisdom" as given in D&C 89 does get specific. Some few Latter-Day Saints read D&C 89:3 and see an invitation try to figure out how to expand the list of "don'ts" in the Word of Wisdom and brow-beat everyone who will listen into accepting their brain-farts as gospel. That is the very opposite of what was intended. Originally the Word of Wisdom was accepted as it was intended as described in verse 2, "To be sent greeting; not by commandment or constraint, but by revelation and the word of wisdom,". But it didn't take long for the Saints to find reasons to, by the voice of the conference, make it binding on the membership of the Church.

Read D&C 89 for yourself and you will find reasons to sympathize with the idea that it wasn't meant to be made binding and reasons to believe it should be made binding. For me the proof is in the pudding or in this case, the wheat and hot drinks. Wheat is recommended for man's consumption, but a large minority of people are allergic to wheat. The "hot drinks" forbidden by the Word of Wisdom have been interpreted as coffee and tea. There are many studies showing benefits from drinking both. The alternative medicine crowd give high marks for the benefits of green tea, although I have run across one doctor with knowledge of a study which shows that some people can show unwanted side effects. Personally, I sometimes wonder if it would have been better if Joseph had never received the Word of Wisdom. Perhaps fewer people would imagine that if they follow their doctor's orders and refrain from partaking of coffee, tea, tobacco, and alcohol they don't have any further need to concern themselves about matters of health. Or, perhaps things would have turned out worse. In the mean-time traditional medicine is taking far too many victims and becoming far too costly as folks blindly allow their health insurance to pay for whatever expensive treatments their doctor proscribes instead of taking a personal interest in and some responsibility for their own health.

As an example of the many failures of traditional medicine I am including a copy of an article I wrote for my blog:

VITAMIN "D" AND DR. WHITAKER — "ARE THE SPOKESMEN FOR TRADITIONAL MEDICINE ENCOURAGING WINTERTIME VITAMIN D DEFICIENCY FOR SOME DEVIOUS PURPOSE?" DR. WHITAKER STATES THE CASE FOR HIGHER RECOMMENDED DAILY ALLOWANCES.

My comments on information taken from Dr. Whitaker's "Health and Healing" newsletter of January, 2012, vol. 22, No.1

I admire Dr. Whitaker for the information he brings us. I found the January, 2012 issue to be especially scary with regards to the difference between what traditional medicine recommends and what studies show. If you live in the tropics you may not be interested in what the doctor has to say. For the rest of us Dr. Whitaker catches our attention with the following, "The primary source of this very important vitamin is ultraviolet radiation from sunlight, which stimulates the synthesis of vitamin D in the skin. During the summer, if you spent just 20 minutes in the midday sun in a bathing suit, you would generate about 10,000 IU of vitamin D. In wintertime, however, you could sunbathe nude on the Sears Tower in Chicago and not generate any at all. The angle of the sun plus absorption by the atmosphere prevents penetration of the UV rays that produce vitamin D."

Dr. Whitaker's complaints against the guidelines on vitamin D are that they appear to only be about the importance of the vitamin to bone health. In 2010, according to Dr. Whitaker, the Food and Nutrition Board of the Institute of Medicine issued new guidelines on vitamin D which ignore "tens of thousands of studies showing the protective effects of vitamin D against heart disease, cancer, autoimmune disease, type 1 and type 2 diabetes, and more." Later on he also lists multiple sclerosis, influenza, falls and fractures, and several specific cancers.

The doctor finds it amazing that the "tolerable upper limit" of vitamin D was set at 4,000 IU daily for adults in spite of the fact that they could find no evidence of harm in taking up to 10,000 IU of vitamin D. He points out that between 1955 and 1990 all East German babies received more than 4,000 IU from birth through 18 months of age without any reports of vitamin D toxicity. He also notes that at the time of reunification with West Germany, the East German children were surprisingly healthy despite substandard living conditions.

Doctor Whitaker continues his attack on low dosage Vitamin D as leaving children susceptible to type 1 diabetes by pointing out the differences in the statistics for children in different climes. In Rochester, Minnesota 22 per 100,000 are affected, 3 per 100,000 in San Diego, California and virtually none in Cuba. However, he points to Finland as providing the most dramatic example of experience with different dosages of vitamin D. "In 1964, the recommended daily intake of vitamin D for children in Finland was inexplicably reduced from 4,500 to 2,000 IU, and the number of children with type 1 diabetes began to rise. In 1975, the prescribed dosage was lowered to 1,000 IU, and disease rates climbed higher. In 1992, it was cut again, this time to 400 IU, and incidence skyrocketed. Today, Finland has one of the world's highest rates of this devastating disease."

I find it very strange that bureaucrats the world over are willing to push prescription drugs our way which have known adverse side effects, but are almost unanimously against crediting nutritional supplements with the ability to improve health or prevent disease. Dr. Whitaker is confident that 5,000 IU of supplemental vitamin D3 per day can safely elevate your blood level of vitamin D into the protective range. He's talking about reducing the incidence of cancer by 35 %, eliminating two thirds of all new diagnoses of type 1 diabetes, halving the number of people afflicted with multiple sclerosis, and preventing 50 percent of all fractures or you can follow the Food and Nutrition Board's lead and take 600 IU. "All I can say is do so at your own risk." Dr. Whitaker lists some references for those wishing more information and his article notes the blood levels of vitamin D in question.

For more health advice and solutions visit www.drwhitaker.com. I recommend reading *FDA* for further reading on the dangers of placing all your hopes for the cure of disease on practitioners of traditional medicine alone:

Probably for decades the drinking of caffeinated soft drinks was a controversial issue in the Church. There was always someone trying to expand the list of "don'ts". While I was serving in the Southern States Mission we got wind of something that occurred in a neighboring mission. It seems that the missionaries were teaching their converts that they had to refrain from drinking caffeinated soft drinks so Franklin D. Richards stopped by their mission office to straighten them out. Elder Richards invited the mission leaders to come with him to a soda fountain where he treated each of them to a cola drink. In order to maintain a clear conscience before God, Latter-Day Saints would be well advised to live the Word of Wisdom.

I also obtain many of my herbs, vitamins, and minerals from Swanson Health Products.

CHAPTER 5

NAUVOO

In D&C 63:31 the saints were warned that failure to settle in Missouri would result in their being scourged from city to city. With the failure of the Saints to settle in Missouri they gathered to the village of Commerce, Illinois and renamed it Nauvoo. September 11, 1836 was the set time for the redemption of Zion, but it didn't happen. Instead those who did make the attempt to settle there faced brutal persecution, and by October 27, 1838 Lilburn W. Boggs, Governor of Missouri had issued an extermination order against the Mormons. The slaughter of Latter-Day Saints at Haun's Mill was disgraceful. Additionally, Parley P. Pratt claimed that 1,200 souls were driven from Missouri. On January 19, 1841 Joseph received a revelation, D&C 124, concerning the building up of Nauvoo. Selected verses will follow;

> 27) ...build a house unto my name, for the Most High to dwell therein.
> 45) And if my people will hearken unto my voice, and unto the voice of my servants whom I have appointed to lead my people, behold, verily I say unto you, they shall not be moved out of their place.
> 47) And it shall come to pass that if you build a house unto my name, and do not the things that I say, I will not perform the

oath which I make unto you, neither fulfill the promises which ye expect at my hands, saith the Lord.

48) For instead of blessings, ye, by your own works, bring cursings, wrath, indignation, and judgments upon your own heads, by your follies, and by all your abominations, which you practise before me, saith the Lord."

The Lord then gives them some consolation concerning their failure to redeem Zion.

49) Verily, verily, I say unto you, that when I give a commandment to any of the sons of men to do a work unto my name, and those sons of men go with all their might and with all they have to perform that work, and cease not their diligence, and their enemies come upon them and hinder them from performing that work, behold, it behooveth me to require that work no more at the hands of those sons of men, but to accept of their offerings.

53) And this I make an example unto you, for your consolation concerning all those who have been commanded to do a work and have been hindered by the hands of their enemies, and by oppression, saith the Lord your God.

54) For I am the Lord your God, and will save all those of your brethren who have been pure in heart, and have been slain in the land of Missouri, saith the Lord."

It was all too obvious to the Saints what they had lost. They lost the chance to lay the foundation of the New Jerusalem. All that remained was the honor of telling of things to come and where the New Jerusalem would be built. The result of their failure was that they would be driven from city to city, but they were given another chance in Nauvoo.

55) And again, verily I say unto you, I command you again to build a house to my name, even in this place, that you may prove yourselves unto me that I may bless you, and crown you with honor, immortality, and eternal life."

Of Nauvoo and her people a Mr. Babbitt is reported by the Nauvoo Neighbor to have said, on March 5th, 1845 (CHC Vol. 2 p. 485); "... a large and respectable city has sprung up in four years containing about 12,000 inhabitants-that farms have been improved and made productive-that manufactories have commenced-a rich and growing trade encouraged, and wealth increased by the rapid development of the national resources of our country. Perhaps he does not know that the 'Mormon' citizens of our state are engaged in the common associations of life-that they like other men-are honest and industrious in their pursuit after happiness and wealth. Yet sir, his ignorance of the fact, makes it no less true. For increase of population and advancement in wealth, the 'Mormon' city of Nauvoo is without parallel in the annals of our country. It has become the object of universal notice and admiration. It has excited the curiosity of the civilized world."

Nauvoo became an incorporated city by act of state legislature in the closing month of 1840. In accordance with the city charter an ordinance was passed on February 3rd, 1841 authorizing the organization of the Nauvoo legion. The Nauvoo Legion was organized as part of the Illinois state militia. Governor Thomas Carlin commissioned Joseph to be lieutenant general of the Nauvoo legion and to take that rank from February 5th, 1841. Until the charter of the city of Nauvoo and the Nauvoo legion were repealed in January of 1845 by the Illinois state legislature, it played an important role in providing for the safety of the citizens of Nauvoo. That same month of 1845 the state's attorney, Josiah Lamborn, wrote an apologetic letter to Brigham Young, CHC Vol. 2, p. 468-469; "I have always considered that your enemies have been prompted by political and religious prejudices, and by a desire for plunder and blood, more than the common good. By the repeal of your charter, and by refusing all amendments and modifications, our legislature has given a kind of sanction to the barbarous manner in which you have been treated. Your two representatives exerted themselves to the extent of their ability in your behalf, but the tide of popular passion and frenzy was to strong to be resisted. It is truly a melancholy spectacle to witness the lawmakers of a sovereign state condescending to pander to the vices, ignorance and malevolence of a class of people who are at all times ready for riot, murder and rebellion."

When in 1845 the Saints were deprived of the protection of the Nauvoo legion, its charter having been repealed, every low-life looking for easy pickings came to Nauvoo. It was in this time of danger, that the whistling and whittling brigade was formed. Groups of small boys would gather around a suspected or undesirable stranger. Armed with jackknives or bowie knives and sticks they gather around him whistling and whittling, but speaking not a word until he would become frustrated and leave town.

During their stay in Nauvoo the Saints were under a temporary reprieve from the penalty of their past failures, the penalty of being driven from city to city, of which they had some experience already, having been driven from New York, from Ohio, and Missouri. In the October conference of 1841 Joseph told the Saints that they would have no more General Conferences until they could meet in the Nauvoo Temple, H.C., Vol. 2, p. 426. This was not only incentive for the Saints to finish the Temple, it was also a temporary deprivation of their authority to judge on matters of the business of the Church.

Until the Saints were deprived of meeting in general conference, as far as I can tell, the rights they enjoyed were as described by Brigham Young in Great Salt Lake City, October 6, 1855, JD, Vol. 3, p.44; "They [the Saints] are to judge not only men, they are to be judges not only in the capacity of a Conference to decide what shall be done, what course shall be pursued to further the kingdom of God, what business shall be transacted, and how it shall be transacted, and so on…"

So, telling the Saints that they would not meet in conference until they could meet in the Temple was no small matter for according to D&C 64:37-39;

- 37) Behold, I, the lord, have made my church in these last days like unto a judge sitting on a hill, in a high place, to judge the nations.
- 38) For it shall come to pass that the inhabitants of Zion shall judge all things pertaining to Zion.
- 39) And liars and hypocrites shall be proved by them, and they who are not apostles and prophets shall be known."

The Saints were told in D&C 105:5 that "Zion cannot be built up unless it is by the principles of the law of the celestial kingdom...", and they were told wherein they had failed. In an earlier chapter it was explained why I believe that the gentile saints had already doomed themselves to failure in the effort to build the New Jerusalem. That failure was, in my opinion, their refusal to allow blacks of African descent to hold the priesthood. In Nauvoo something perhaps even more monstrous came to light and doomed the effort to remain there. For it was there that the specter of polygamy resulted in the death of the prophet. They were warned in D&C 124:48; "For instead of blessings, ye, by your own works, bring cursings, wrath, indignation, and judgments upon your own heads, by your follies, and by all your abominations, which you practise before me, saith the Lord."

In the Book of Mormon, the Book of Jacob, chapter 2:23-30, the Lord clearly describes polygamy as an abomination;

> 23) ...This people begin to wax in iniquity; they understand not the scriptures, for they seek to excuse themselves in committing whoredoms, because of the things which were written concerning David, and Solomon his son.
> 24) Behold, David and Solomon truly had many wives and concubines, which thing was abominable before me, saith the Lord.
> 25) Wherefore, thus saith the Lord, I have led this people forth out of the land of Jerusalem, by the power of mine arm, that I might raise up unto me a righteous branch from the fruit of the loins of Joseph.
> 26) Wherefore, I the Lord God will not suffer that this people shall do like unto them of old.
> 27) Wherefore, my brethren, hear me, and hearken to the word of the Lord: For there shall not any man among you have save it be one wife; and concubines he shall have none;
> 28) For I, the Lord God, delight in the chastity of women. And whoredoms are an abomination before me; thus saith the Lord of Hosts.

29) Wherefore, this people shall keep my commandments, saith the lord of Hosts, or cursed be the land for their sakes.
30) For if I will, saith the Lord of Hosts, raise up seed unto me, I will command my people; otherwise they shall hearken unto these things."

Verses 25-29 explain why the Lord commanded the Nephites to refrain from committing whoredoms, it was because He wanted to raise up a righteous branch. D&C 100:16 explains that the Lord wanted the Church to become a "pure people, that will serve me in righteousness." So in verse 30 of Jacob 2 the last phrase says "otherwise they shall hearken unto these things." Which things will they hearken to and what will He command His people if He wants to raise up seed unto himself? Brigham Young would have us believe that verse 30 contradicts the previous verses in providing for an exception. If you believe verses 23-29 it would be logical to believe that the Lord is just repeating Himself, not making an exception, and it should be understood to mean "For if I will raise up righteous seed unto me, I will command my people to have only one wife and no concubines; otherwise they will hearken unto the things which David and Solomon did."

But, let me remind the reader that you don't have to be a polygamist in order to lust after other men's wives and commit adultery in your heart. Polygamy was an accepted practice during Abraham's day and the Lord did not ask him to avoid that lifestyle. Were we to have a greater understanding of the customs, culture, and economy of that day we might not wonder why it was allowed. Perhaps the Lord is more accepting of sins of ignorance, and necessity, and more patient than we might imagine.

Though Joseph denied having more than one wife, there have been serious efforts to make a liar of him. Those efforts increased in Nauvoo and the rumors culminated in an article in the Nauvoo Expositor. When Joseph destroyed the press which produced the Nauvoo Expositor the public outcry resulted in his incarceration and death as a mob stormed the jail.

From a major library I obtained a copy of the Nauvoo Expositor. From that first and only issue of the Nauvoo Expositor which caused so much trouble; June 7th, 1844:

"To whom it may Concern:

Forasmuch as the public mind hath been much agitated by a course of procedure in the Church of Jesus Christ of Latter-Day Saints, by a number of persons declaring against certain doctrines and practices therein, (among whom I am one,) it is but meet that I should give my reasons, at least in part, as a cause that hath led me to declare myself. In the latter part of the summer, 1843, the Patriarch, Hyrum Smith, did in the High Council, of which I was a member, introduce what he said was a revelation given through the Prophet; that the said Hyrum Smith did essay to read the said revelation in the said Council, that according to this reading there was contained the following doctrines; 1st. The sealing up of persons to eternal life, against all sins, save that of shedding innocent blood or of consenting thereto, 2nd. The doctrine of a plurality of wives, or marrying virgins; that David and Solomon had many wives, yet in this they sinned not save in the matter of Uriah. This revelation with other evidence, that the aforesaid heresies were taught and practiced in the Church; determined me to leave the office of first counselor to the president of the Church at Nauvoo, inasmuch as I dared not teach or administer such laws. And further deponent saith not.

AUSTIN COWLES.

State of Illinois, \'7d To all whom it may concern
Hancock County, \'7d ss.

I hereby certify that the above certificate was sworn and subscribed before me, this fourth day of May, 1844.

ROBERT D. FOSTER, J. P."

The things claimed to be in the revelation which Austin Cowles says was read to the High Council are indeed in Section 132. However, polygamy was not an acceptable practice in the western world and D&C

49:16 reaffirmed the idea that a man should have but one wife. D&C 107:84 stipulates that "none shall be exempted from the justice and the laws of God...." But, it is clear that D&C 132 or something like it was in existence in the 1840s. In the introduction of HC Vol. 5, pp. XXIX -XLVI you will find testimonies and arguments supporting the idea that Joseph was the author of D&C 132 and that he had practiced polygamy as early 1831 according to Orson Pratt for one. In addition to testimony of several of the leading brethren the arguments also rely on unproven accusations by enemies, where there is smoke there is fire, and arguments based on the nature of the text of D&C 132.

William Clayton, was appointed the temple recorder and also the recorder of Joseph's revelations on the 7th of April, 1842. On the 12th of July, 1843 Brother Clayton claims he transcribed the revelation on plural marriage as Joseph dictated. Joseph C. Kingsbury made a copy of it and also testified that he knew of Joseph marrying other women besides his first wife, Emma, and he named several of them. See CHC Vol. 2, p.106-107. The revelation on plural marriage, D&C 132, is found in the Joseph Smith History of the Church because it was at a later time inserted there. It was not found in Joseph's journals including the journal William Clayton kept as Joseph's scribe in Nauvoo.

According to p.XXXII in the introduction to HC Vol. 5, William Clayton gave the copy to Hyrum Smith who gave it back to Joseph after showing it to Joseph's wife, Emma. Joseph then lent it to Joseph C. Kingsbury who made a copy. Joseph took the original home, but Emma made such a fuss over it that he gave it to her so she could tear it up. The copy was preserved by Bishop Whitney and according to p.XXXIII nothing more was heard of it until the temporary camps of Israel were located in Winter Quarters on the Missouri River in 1846. It is difficult to find anything about polygamy in the Joseph Smith History of the Church which wasn't placed there as sworn testimony by someone else. Apparently, either Joseph was keeping his polygamous endeavors out of his journals or they just didn't happen and all those testimonies are lies.

In a footnote on page 97 of volume 2 of CHC, B.H. Roberts testifies as to the noble purpose of plural marriage in the Church describing it as a sacrament and not intended to be a general practice of the saints. Only men of the most worthy status were to indulge. They want us to believe that they could ignore the warning in the Book of Mormon if they carefully controlled the practice of Polygamy. On the other hand, the need to justify the assertions that Joseph had been practicing polygamy since 1831 has led to the popularizing of the idea that if Joseph did it there is no doubt that it was right and proper. Another ploy is a rumor popular in some circles that "If you become righteous enough some day you will be asked to do something which was previously thought to be evil."

Once they were openly practicing polygamy in Utah, Brigham Young clearly stated his beliefs on the subject. JD Vol. 16, p.166, "Now, where a man in this church says, 'I don't want but one wife, I will live my religion with one,' he will perhaps be saved in the celestial kingdom; but when he gets there he will not find himself in possession of any wife at all."

Before leaving Nauvoo, Brigham Young supervised the revision of Joseph's history. Brigham Young reported an instance of sealing a woman to Joseph in Nauvoo during a gathering at Paris, Idaho on August 31st, 1873. JD, Vol.16, p.166-167; "I recollect a sister conversing with Joseph Smith on this subject. She told him: 'Now, don't talk to me; when I get into the celestial kingdom, if I ever do get there, I shall request the privilege of being a ministering angel; that is the labor that I want to perform. I don't want any companion in that world; and if the Lord will make me a ministering angel, it is all I want.' Joseph said, 'Sister, you talk very foolishly, you do not know what you will want.' He then said to me: 'Here, brother Brigham, you seal this lady to me.' I sealed her to him. This was my own sister according to the flesh." So, according to Brigham Young, he sealed his own sister to Joseph, but this sounds to me like a widow or spinster who wasn't interested in Joseph as a husband in heaven or on earth.

Instead of producing a pure people they created an elitist subculture within the church. A clique of pious snobs who believe "that if you are righteous enough you may be asked to do something which was previously thought to be evil." I heard such whisperings before I left the Church thirty years ago. Someone was also telling the single adult sisters that they were not as responsible for sexual misconduct as men were. These people are a rarity in the Church because they are likely to join the Fundamentalists, take on extra wives and get caught and kicked out of the Church. They are obsessed with polygamy and have such sensitive feelings for sisters who have less active or non-member husbands that they long for polygamy in heaven where they can add the sister to their harem. These are not the brethren who will help a brother who is having trouble with his testimony for they instinctively try to push him further away from the Church so that they might have a chance to add his wife to their harem in the Celestial Kingdom. That kind of brethren have been in my face and behind my back watching for opportunities to push me away.

Was Joseph Smith a lying bigamist? If he was he certainly paid the price with his life's blood. If he wasn't, he may have somehow encouraged some of the leaders in that direction in order to insure that the Church was properly driven and scourged from city to city until they were removed from the vicinity of the "Center Place". When the Lord decides to bring the tribe of Joseph to build the New Jerusalem it would not likely be a good idea to be in the way of that effort. I suspect that Joseph knew that he was an instrument in the hands of the Lord in testing the Saints. He brought the Pearl of Great Price to the Saints which helped them to justify their discrimination against blacks. There is evidence that he at least encouraged the Saints to think that polygamy was okay even if the evidence that he was a bigamist is a frame up. HC, Vol. 6, p.441, Joseph complained; "They make it a criminality for a man to have a wife on the earth while he has one in heaven, according to the keys of the Holy Priesthood;" This sounds to me like Joseph had wives or a wife sealed to him only for eternity while Emma was his for time and eternity. So the question remains; were the extra wives Joseph was reported to have sealed to him merely sealed to him for the after life? I find it hard to believe that Joseph was a liar. I find it easier to believe that those marriages he is accused of were not consummated. This view allows us to see Joseph and the brethren accusing him of having extra wives as only being guilty of spin rather than being outright liars.

The public and official announcement of the practice of plural marriage was made at a special conference held in Salt Lake City on the 28th and 29th of August, 1852. This, after several years of rumors that the leading elders of the church were practicing polygamy. But, the early brethren in Utah were not merely justifying their own practice of polygamy, they were also fighting legal battles for the right to claim to be the original Church of Jesus of Latter-Day Saints against claims for that title by the Reorganized Church of Jesus Christ of Latter-Day Saints. Even a small group called the Hedrikites or Church of Christ -Temple Lot were involved in claims for Church property and they obtained title to 1/3rd of the Temple site in Independence, Missouri. The Reorganized Church of Jesus Christ of Latter-Day Saints obtained title to 1/3rd and we received title to the final third.

For the first two or three years of my apostasy, I was an active member of the Reorganized Church and heard their side of arguments for their rights to church property. As I recall, this included property in Nauvoo, Kirtland, and Independence, Missouri including one third of the temple lot for the New Jerusalem. There may have been other properties involved in the law suits. RLDS arguments relied heavily on testimony that Brigham Young was the author of D&C 132, the revelation on polygamy. So the question must be considered; did the LDS Church overstate the case for Joseph being a polygamist in order to strengthen their case against the claims of the Reorganized Church of Jesus Christ of Latter-Day Saints? They certainly made a great effort to turn Joseph's denials of being a polygamist into bold faced lies.

I dropped out of activity in the Reorganized Church when it became apparent that their leadership and scholars were more interested in becoming popular with the news media than they were in sticking up for the unique claims Joseph Smith made to having been authorized by God, Jesus, and angelic messengers to restore the Church of Jesus Christ anew.

The Saints did not get to stay in Nauvoo, but they did take with them instructions to go forth in the spirit of Elijah in order to perform vicarious ordinances for the departed spirits of their ancestors. Baptism for the dead is one of the ordinances performed in Mormon temples. Baptism for the remission of sins is performed on the living in baptismal fonts in our chapels, or in swimming pools, lakes and rivers. The Savior, being sinless, was baptized to fulfill all righteousness. The Book of Mormon makes it clear that the blood of Christ atones for the sins of those who die not knowing the will of Christ or those who ignorantly sin. But, the Book of Mormon also makes it clear that when we are taught the gospel, we are no more blameless. Therefore when the spirits of those who die without the gospel hear it preached to them they need to accept vicarious baptism performed by the living in their behalf when they recognize their need to repent of the evil desires of their hearts. If by some rare instance they don't have any evil desires of their hearts, they need to accept vicarious baptisms performed in their behalf in order to fulfill all righteousness just as our sinless Lord did when He began his earthly ministry.

Our temples have a baptismal font which bears considerable resemblance to the sea in Solomon's temple which sat upon twelve oxen. The burnt offerings were washed in lavers and the sea was where the priests washed (2Chronicles 4:6). The font in our temples, which also sits on twelve oxen, is used for vicarious baptisms for the dead. We are baptized for our departed ancestors and when the gospel is preached to them in the spirit world they are free to accept or reject the vicarious baptism we perform in their behalf. In the Bible (1st Peter 3:18-20), Peter tells us that after Jesus died on the cross, while he was still in the spirit, He went to the spirit prison to preach the gospel to those who perished during the flood. The last verse of the Old Testament Book of Malachi tells how Elijah would come in the last days to "turn the heart of the fathers to the children, and the heart of the children to their fathers, lest I come and smite the earth with a curse."

April 3rd, 1836, Elijah came to authorize and instruct Joseph Smith in the performing of vicarious temple ordinances for the dead. When people die before God has finished striving with them, they are taught the gospel in the place where departed spirits of those who have not accepted the fullness of the gospel go. As the gospel is preached to those in this world of spirits, they are given a vision of our efforts and sacrifices to do vicarious temple work for them. That imparted knowledge of our efforts in their behalf works upon their hearts and helps to awaken in them a desire to be united with us. This desire aids in their acceptance of the Lord's plan. As we work with aunts, uncles, and cousins to discover our ancestors we uncover a larger and larger list of them and their other living relatives. The bonds of kinship will foster bonds of love among decent folks the world over and make it unnecessary for the Lord to smite the whole earth with the curse mentioned in the last verse of Malachi. Just how much of the earth will be cursed remains to be seen.

The Saints were warned that if they did not finish the Nauvoo Temple on time that they and their dead would be damned. Their enemies prevented them from being able to stay and enjoy it, but some stayed behind to finish the job. There is a bit of a controversy over that claim, and not all of the controversy comes from the testimony of the Reorganized Church. However, I see no need to get in an argument about what George Q. Cannon meant in his conflicting statements from 1871 and 1884. Besides, the Lord previously gave the Saints precedent for wiggle room when enemies interfered in the case of their failure to establish themselves in Missouri. That precedent should cover their failure to finish the Nauvoo Temple before they left, if indeed they did fail to finish it.

Though the Saints left their temple in Nauvoo to be destroyed by their enemies, they took with them a new design which was quite different from their Kirtland edifice. Unlike the Kirtland Temple, the Nauvoo temple had some similarities to the ancient Israelite temples. Just to keep it simple, lets say that they both had a veil and a font sitting on twelve oxen.

The Israelite temple was off-limits to the stranger and to Israelites who were not physically perfect specimens. Isaiah looked forward to a day which was not possible under the Law of Moses. Isaiah 56:3-7, "Neither let the son of the stranger, that hath joined himself to the Lord, speak, saying, The Lord hath utterly separated me from his people: neither let the eunuch say, Behold, I am a dry tree. For thus saith the Lord unto the eunuchs that keep my sabbaths, and choose the things that please me, and take hold of my covenant; Even unto them will I give in mine house and within my walls a better place and a name better than of sons and daughters; I will give them an everlasting name, that shall not be cut off. Also the sons of the stranger, that join themselves to the Lord, to serve him, and to love the name of the Lord, to be his servants, every one that keepeth the Sabbath from polluting it, and taketh hold of my covenant; even them will I bring to my holy mountain, and make them joyful in my house of prayer: their sacrifices shall be accepted upon mine altar; for mine house shall be called an house of prayer for all people." The LDS Church is building temples all around the world. Every worthy adult member can enter our temples. Worthy young members can enter to be baptized for the dead. The day which Isaiah looked forward to is at hand.

The Saints also took with them a new temple endowment. However, there remains some suspicion about the need for secret stuff in our temples. When confronted on that matter, church leaders replied, "It is sacred, not secret." When I returned to the church after 25 years of apostasy I was pleasantly surprised to find that the penalties for revealing sacred things had been removed from the endowment. Seeing as how Jesus told his followers not to make oaths and Joseph Smith also spoke against them I sometimes wondered why they were in the endowment. Oaths were popular among the ancient Israelites, but we know what the Lord thought of that practice if we read a few verses beyond that Matthew quote on divorce. Joseph Smith's thoughts on the subject are also of interest. HC vol. III p. 303, In a March 1839 letter from Liberty Jail we read. "And again, I would further suggest the impropriety of the organization of bands or companies, by covenant or oaths, by penalties or secrecies; but let the time past of our experience and sufferings by the Wickedness of Dr. Avard suffice and let our covenant be that of the Everlasting Covenant, as is contained in the Holy Writ and the things that God hath revealed unto us. Pure friendship always becomes weakened the very moment you undertake to make it stronger by penal oaths and secrecy."

So who placed the penalties in the endowment in the first place? I, for one, am glad they are gone. They encouraged feelings of pious snobbery and a tendency to unrighteous dominion which sometimes and in some places infected the Saints. Those tendencies have not altogether deserted us.

It is to the good report of the saints that the above mentioned Dr. Avard did not gain a stronger following among them. Pages 180-181 of the H.C. reveal his instructions to his captains. "My brethren, as you have been chosen to be our leading men, our captains to rule over this last kingdom of Jesus Christ—and you have been organized after the ancient order—I have called upon you here today to teach you, and instruct you in the things that pertain to your duty, and to show you what your privileges are, and what they soon will be. ..."

Sampson Avard was convinced that he had won such strong loyalty that he could reveal to his captains his plans to rob and plunder the Gentiles. All of his captains revolted once Avard had revealed his true plans so they came to naught, except to give the church a bad name as he blamed the presidency for the organization of the Danites as he had called them. In the first vol. of the CHC on page 503 we see that Avard had given his band secret signs by which they could recognize each other by day or night and they made blood oaths against the revealing of their plans.

As to who was responsible for the penal oaths, it has been assumed by some that Joseph placed them in the endowment because of his association with the Masons. However, I have no way of knowing whether they were even in the endowment given at Nauvoo. Of that endowment Brigham Young said (JD Vol. 2, p.32) on April 6th, 1853 at a ceremony for laying the south east cornerstone of the Salt Lake Temple, "But what of the temple in Nauvoo?... the saints ... so far completed the Temple, despite the devices of the mob, that many received a small portion of their endowment, but we know of no one who received it in its fullness."

Actually, Joseph began to introduce the endowment in the upper floor of his brick store in May of 1842 (CHC, Vol. 2, p. 135). If Brigham Young truly sealed his sister to Joseph in Nauvoo then they must have received as much of the endowment as most saints receive. I haven't even heard of enough beyond the sealing mentioned to justify calling that which includes the sealing a "small portion" of their endowment. So, what was Brigham Young planning on adding which would lead him to say such a thing? Whatever-the-case, I have no problems with changes in the endowment as it is largely symbolism and information designed to encourage us to come to Christ.

Joseph knew that the Saints would be forced to flee to the West. Even Jeremiah of Old Testament times saw them driven to the Salt Lake Valley. Jeremiah 17:5-7, "Thus saith the Lord; Cursed be the man that trusteth in man, and maketh flesh his arm and whose heart departeth from the Lord. For he shall be like the heath in the desert, and shall not see when good cometh; but shall inhabit the parched places in the wilderness, in a salt land and not inhabited." That the Lord allowed them to make the desert blossom testifies to the fact that the Lord did not altogether cast them off. But, will we ever overcome those temptations which cost the saints such serious setbacks? There is still a great deal of fascination with polygamy in the Church.

CHAPTER 6

THE MORMON CHURCH TODAY

When I was about 18 and just beginning to have some doubts about the Baptist Church, some Mormon friends invited me to study their church. They actively believed things in the New Testament which Baptists didn't talk about like baptism for the dead, the three degrees of glory and Jesus being the express image of His Father. Contemplating God as a distinct personage with some kind of glorified body and in possession of personality, He become much more real to me and the thought of becoming like Jesus, as it says in the New Testament, seemed much more possible. Philippians 3:20-21;

20) For our conversation is in heaven: from whence also we look for the Savior, the Lord Jesus Christ:

21) Who shall change our vile body, that it may be fashioned like unto his glorious body, according to the working whereby he is able even to subdue all things unto himself."

It is quite common for Christians to look upon Adam and Eve being kicked out of the garden of Eden as the result of sexual transgression and to feel that the human race was cheated out of the chance to live a utopian existence in the garden of Eden. The Book of Mormon explains that it was necessary for Adam and Eve to leave the garden of

Eden in order to come to know joy and sorrow. As Latter-Day Saints, we believe that we existed as spirits before we came to the Earth to gain mortal bodies and continue to grow and progress. We also have beliefs concerning continued growth and progress in heaven. One of my favorite Book of Mormon verses is found in 2nd Nephi 2:25. It reads," Adam fell that man might be; man is, that he might have joy." We do not define joy as coming from a total lack of struggle or opposition.

Far too many people look at this mortal existence as a huge burden. They see life through the prism of disappointment in Adam's and Eve's loss of paradise. It is the result of becoming obsessed with coveting the possessions of others. It changed my life greatly to look at mortality as an opportunity to grow and prepare for continued growth in eternity. Our Father in Heaven did not want us to become lazy slugs hanging around the Garden of Eden where all we had to do was pick our food off the trees with no other concerns. The evolutionists that I read also believe in progress through struggle and challenge.

While Latter-Day Saints believe in "earning our bread by the sweat of our brow", we also believe in taking care of the needy. Recipients of church welfare are given assignments to work at Church canneries, farms, or Bishops Storehouses so that they can feel like they are contributing to the cost of the help they receive. All the members of the Church who are capable are also given opportunities to have a turn at helping out at canneries, farms and storehouses which they happily do knowing that it is for the benefit of those who need help. So when you vote a Mormon into office you are likely electing someone who believes in helping others, but not in such a way that the recipients of welfare are deprived of their pride or their sense of obligation to be contributing members of society. When you vote for a Mormon you are voting for someone who believes in getting personally involved with helping the poor by doing more than simply paying his taxes. He or she, if fully active, pays tithing, fast offerings, and contributes to other funds in addition to accepting assignments at Church farms, canneries, storehouses, and voluntarily helping his neighbors without being asked. All that after working for a living, paying taxes, and perhaps being active in the community.

Latter-Day Saints also believe in serving their country. Mormons serve in every branch of our military. We believe that the founders of our great nation were inspired by God in establishing our Constitution and Bill of Rights. And yes, we believe in getting married and having children, preferably more than one. There is no greater responsibility than being a parent. I believe it was the Mormon prophet David O. McKay who said, "No success can compensate for failure in the home".

Please allow me to present a narrative of things I have gleaned from our scriptures and traditions. I do not necessarily agree with everything which is popularly believed by my fellow Mormons, but I certainly don't believe the oversimplified sectarian view that we must accept the gospel in mortality to obtain heaven or suffer in hell for eternity. If you are disposed to call any additional details mythology you might as well throw most of the Bible away, for much of what follows can be seen there. I'm asking for the chance to have some clarity on the subject of where we came from, why we are here and where we are going. What follows is my slant on Latter-Day Saint beliefs.

In the first chapter of Genesis we learn of God's power to plan and create. Through verse 25 it was, let there be this and let there be that, let this happen and let that happen. In verse 26 we see something new;

> 26) And God said, Let us make man in our image, after our likeness: and let them have dominion over the fish of the sea, and over the fowl of the air, and over the cattle, and over all the earth, and over every creeping thing that creepeth upon the earth.
> 27) So God created man in his own image, in the image of God created he him; male and female created he them."

So, when it comes to planning how to make man, an "us" and an "our" enters into the picture. Furthermore, the Creator has a form which we resemble and there is included in the realm of deity, female "us" which some of mankind are to be made in the image of.

In chapter 3:22 we learn something else about God; "And the Lord God said, Behold, the man is become as one of us, to know good and evil:" We learn that God has a code of ethics and He had them before Adam and Eve came upon the scene. The thing that radical atheists hate most about us is that we have standards of right and wrong and some of them are absolute.

Let's proceed on this quest for clarity by setting aside the notion that the reality we are examining is a three act play; a war in Heaven, mortal life on Earth, and Heaven or hell after the final judgment wherein we sit around playing harps and singing praises to God for eternity or burn forever in hell. Picture with me those three acts as merely a glimpse of a single segment of a never ending story about creation.

As to the eternal nature of God, Joseph Smith proclaimed that we are all eternal beings having existed as intelligences (whatever that means). The first step in our progression was for God to clothe our intelligence in a body of spirit. He created our spirit bodies in His image and randomly imprinted each of us with different portions of his being while Jesus as the First Born received a fullness. From our earliest existence in that pre-mortal world of spirits we were free to choose and some of us chose to come out against God's plan, a plan which would give us the chance to continue along the path of eternal progression by gaining physical bodies.

The populating of the Earth with God's creations is not an isolated incident. God wants us to be able to join him in His continuing work of creation. We believe in eternal progression for though Jesus was made a little lower than the angels, He learned from his experiences, according to Hebrews 5:8-9;

8) Though he were a Son, yet learned he obedience by the things which He suffered;
9) And being made perfect, He became the author of eternal salvation unto all them that obey him".

Jesus, as He went about his earthly ministry, did what his Father told him. That was not true of all of God's children. God is a just God who wants us to learn to want to be like him of our own free will. You can read more about that in John 5:19-20.

Jesus came to claim his own from among the many who had decided not to follow Satan in the War in Heaven. He came to establish a dividing point, a criteria for determining who would be cast out with the

Devil and his angels after mortality and who would inherit a kingdom of glory. The War in Heaven was fought over Satan's decision to overturn the order of Heaven and take all the glory for himself. God's spirit children had yet to experience dwelling in a physical body and discover whether or not they might be able to resist and control obsessions with animal appetites. They were, in the meantime, getting acquainted with group dynamics and the personal interplay of individuals attempting to influence each other. God had divided them into groups for training and nurture, but they had further divided themselves into groups based on common interests, many of them not in tune with the Father's plan.

Satan (a son of the morning), one of the older spirit children of God thought he had a more appealing plan than God's program to advance us according to our desires and capabilities which we learn about in the Savior's parable of the talents in Matthew chapter 25:14-30;

> 14) For the kingdom of heaven is as a man traveling into a far country, who called his own servants, and delivered unto them his goods.
> 15) An unto one he gave five talents, to another two, and to another one; to every man according to his several ability; and straightway took his journey.
> 16) Then he that had received the five talents went and traded with the same, and made them other five talents.
> 17) And likewise he that had received two, he also gained other two.
> 18) But he that had received one went and digged in the earth, and hid his lords's money.
> 19) After a long time the lord of those servants cometh, and reckoneth with them.
> 20) And so he that had received five talents came and brought other five talents, saying, Lord, thou deliveredst unto me five talents: behold, I have gained beside them five talents more.
> 21) His lord said unto him, Well done, thou good and faithful servant :thou hast been faithful over a few things, I will make thee ruler over many things: enter thou into the joy of thy lord. ..."

You know the rest of the story; the lord said the same thing unto the servant who had received two talents, but from the one who had buried his lord's talent, it was taken and given to the one with ten talents. Lucifer pretended to have a better plan. If the Left had been in charge they would have taken the extra five earned by the first one and given four of them to the one who buried his one talent and to the servant who had two plus two extra for a total of four they would have given one so each of them would have ended up with five. That's how the Left would tell it in order to obtain power, but actually the Left would have shot the one who buried his talent and left the other two with only one or two so that they could use the rest for summer homes on the Black Sea for themselves and to hire servants and entertainers for their own enjoyment.

Lucifer must have been very convincing for he talked one third of the spirits to follow him in outright rebellion when God rejected his plan. They were cast out and came to Earth without receiving bodies of flesh and blood like the rest of us. Our coming to Earth to gain mortal bodies provides a lull in that war which started in Heaven, but those evil spirits are busy whispering in our ears, "It's not fair that someone should have more things than you have." Into the ears of those who are powerful they are whispering, "Mistreat your servants and make them fearful and resentful of you." Thus they hope to make our mortal lives miserable.

The war was not drawn strictly between good and evil but between those who chose to follow Satan (they were very evil) and those who didn't (they were a wide variety of good and evil). Our time on earth provides amnesty for those who sided with Jesus, but weren't fully in tune with God's plan. It's a fresh start for each of us as we come here with no memory of our time as spirits during our pre-mortal existence in Heaven. Meanwhile, the Devil and his angels are very much involved in guerrilla warfare as they attempt to influence us to be evil. Their one hope is to get as many of us as possible to rebel against God thinking that they still have a chance to create a kingdom for themselves wherein they can rule over us.

Jesus took responsibility for those of us who were on his side and not merely against Lucifer, for God promised them to him. Some may have been hesitant to come to Earth and be judged on our performance. He assured us and the Father that He would accept the punishment we deserve for our misdeeds performed during our mortal lives if we would eventually repent and follow him. He agreed to allow himself to be crucified in order to atone for our sins and to show that evil and goodness cannot coexist. It would be a demonstration of the Savior's power over death and Hell and it was a pivotal point in the Father's plan of happiness. For those who eventually accept Jesus the crucifixion provides an atonement for their sins if they truly repent, are baptized, receive the Holy Ghost by the laying on of hands and endure to the end. For those who will not repent the crucifixion provides justification for casting them into Outer Darkness with the Devil and his angels making Heaven the place of happiness it could not be with them to afflict us. God is just so both possibilities must be open to us. He will force no one to accept the requirements for living in one of his kingdoms.

The God I worship does not send decent people to Hell merely because they die before they have the proper opportunity to accept the gospel. He decides when each person has had that chance whether in mortality or the spirit world after they die. If they accept the gospel in the spirit world they will be given the opportunity to accept the vicarious ordinances we perform for the dead in our temples thereby not having to suffer in hell until the final judgment.

I suspect that the very wicked go directly to Hell. All of those who refuse to accept Jesus as their savior during their mortal lives or in the world of spirits after they die, go to hell at least until the final judgment. Those whom the Lord has given up on must suffer punishment for their sins. A search of the four gospels of the Bible will show that Jesus promoted the idea among some that there are varying degrees of punishment depending on the accountability of the sinner and the severity of the sin. John 9:41; "And Jesus said unto them, If ye were blind, ye should have no sin: but now ye say, We see; therefore your sin remaineth." In John 15:22 we find, "If I had not come and spoken unto them, they had not had sin: but now they have no cloke for their sin." In Luke 12:47-48;

47) And that servant, which knew his lord's will, and prepared not himself, neither did according to his will, shall be beaten with many stripes.

48) But he that knew not, and did commit things worthy of stripes, shall be beaten with few stripes, For unto whomsoever much is given, of him shall be much required: and to whom men have committed much, of him they will ask the more."

At the final resurrection and judgment those who are filthy still will be cast out to spend eternity with the Devil and his angels. Those who had the hell burned out of them will be eligible for the lowest kingdom of glory.

Jesus is calling for us to repent. He made it clear that he offers the same wage to all those who answer the call to serve him. Whether in our youth, our middle age or old age He paid the price of our sins when they hung him on the cross. In the sense that He paid for our sins, He has paid us equally for serving him. He also has criteria for assigning us to responsibilities which suit our demonstrated desires and capabilities in the appropriate mansion or kingdom of glory on high as explained previously in the parable of the talents. Family has a purpose during mortality and in heaven will have purpose. Because we believe in the continuation of the family in heaven we have temple ordinances to make that possible. Temple marriage is for sealing husband and wife together. Children are sealed to parents in a ceremony for that purpose.

These are my beliefs as a member of the Church of Jesus Christ of Latter-Day Saints. I further stipulate that I believe the Book of Mormon prediction that it will grow together with the Bible to the putting down of contention and establishing peace. In the meantime, we have similar things going on in the Church which happened in New Testament times. Paul told the Corinthians in Chapter 11:19, "For there must be also heresies among you, that they which are approved may be made manifest among you."

The organization of the church might seem slightly confusing at first to newcomers, but is fairly simple. A congregation constitutes a Ward which is also a geographical area and is presided over by a Bishop who has two counselors to assist him. A ward is usually divided before it reaches over a thousand members and may be well under five hundred members. This way a larger percentage of the members are able to receive callings of responsibility and there are lots of callings. There is a Sunday School Presidency and teachers, a Primary presidency and teachers for young children, for teenage boys there is both a priesthood organization (the Aaronic Priesthood) and a Young Men's organization for activities and instruction which includes the Boy Scouts, and for teenage girls there is a Young Women's organization for activities and instruction. As they become adults the young men are expected to advance in the priesthood to what we call the Melchizedek Priesthood and if it suites their natures to serve full time missions. For adult sisters there is also the possibility of serving full time missions and activity in the Relief Society organization. The Relief Society sisters have similar responsibilities towards their fellow sisters as the Melchizedek Priesthood has toward ward members.

The Wards are grouped into geographical and ecclesiastical units called Stakes. In an area where membership is scarce, instead of a Ward we would have a Branch and a District instead of a Stake. There are other subdivisions with little relevance except for administrative purposes. A Bishop presides over a Ward, and a Stake President over a Stake. A Branch President presides over a Branch and a District President over a District. Each Ward has an Elder's Quorum which includes a presidency and a High Priest's Group which includes group leadership. Each Stake has a High Priest's Quorum. An Elder's Quorum has a Presidency consisting of a President and two counselors. The Stake president and his two counselors preside over the High Priest's Quorum and all the quorums and organizations in a stake. Each stake has a council of twelve High Priests who assist the Stake Presidency in the work of the Stake and sit in judgment when a member's status in the church is called in question and the Bishop of the ward he belongs to has no jurisdiction. Each type of ward organization has a presidency in the stake which is responsible for giving guidance and training to its respective ward leadership. It seems to be a general principle that every presidency consists of a president and two counselors except that the Seventy have seven presidents with no counselors.

The Mormon Church Today

The earthly head of the Church is our prophet who is also the president of the Church as a legal corporation. He has two counselors and a quorum of Twelve Apostles who are also prophets. The other general authorities consist of a Presiding Bishopric and quorums of Seventy. The Church holds two General Conferences per year wherein we are given opportunity to hold up our hands to sustain or not to sustain them. When the Church was smaller and before Joseph Smith suspended conferences, those in attendance conducted the business of the church. At one point Brigham Young told the Saints they still had the same authority in conferences that they always had. Until the Saints were deprived of meeting in general conference, as far as I can tell, the rights they enjoyed were as described by Brigham Young in Great Salt Lake City, October 6, 1855, JD, Vol. 3, p.44; "They [the Saints] are to judge not only men, they are to be judges not only in the capacity of a Conference to decide what shall be done, what course shall be pursued to further the kingdom of God, what business shall be transacted, and how it shall be transacted, and so on..."

Later on in that same talk (p. 45), Brigham Young emphasized the importance of the Saints knowing for themselves that the kingdom was properly organized; "Suppose that the people were heedless, that they manifested no concern with regard to the things of the kingdom of God, but threw the whole burden upon the leaders of the people, saying, 'If the brethren who take charge of matters are satisfied, we are,' this is not pleasing in the sight of the Lord."

"Every man and woman in this kingdom ought to be satisfied with what we do, but they never should be satisfied without asking the Father, in the name of Jesus Christ, whether what we do is right. When you are inspired by the Holy Ghost you can understandingly say, that you are satisfied; and that is the only power that should cause you to exclaim that you are satisfied, for without that you do not know whether you should be satisfied or not." However, Brigham delivered mixed messages regarding the voice of the conference. September 30, 1860 (JD Vol. 8, p. 189), speaking of Joseph Smith, Brigham Young said; "The people required him to be as holy as the Almighty himself, and to never make a mistake. Wherein the First Presidency and the Twelve do wrong, it is not in the ability of the people to detect them in those wrongs. ... if they commit an error, it is passed over, and the people cannot tell wherein or when, or how to correct it."

So, although we may still hold up our hands against sustaining a leader if we know of some serious sin they are guilty of, they do not sustain us as being capable of influencing the business of the Church.

In the early days of the Church the general authorities served full time missions, but the Church has become so large that they have too much to do in the way of supervising the Lord's work to spend time knocking on doors. By the way, our general authorities are the only leaders who are provided a living because of their callings. Our full time missionaries pay their own way though in some cases ward members contribute to help pay their expenses. Young men starting at 18 years of age and young ladies starting at 19 years old are called to serve full time missions. The young men serve for two years and the young ladies for a year and one half. Retired members also serve on full time missions, often for administrative duties. At the time I was writing the first draft of this book the ward I live in had two retired couples serving full time missions, one in South America, and the other in a former Iron Curtain country. We also had one young lady serving in Central America, a young man in Japan, one in Nebraska, a young man in South America, and five more have been called recently. Of the recent calls one went to Australia and the others are serving stateside or soon will. Fifty years ago, I served two years in what was then the Southern States Mission consisting of Georgia, Alabama, and South Carolina.

CHAPTER 7

MY PERSONAL STORY

I was only six years old when mom and dad moved to California with me and my two sisters so my memories of those years on the farm are scarce and hazy. I remember watching a velvet ant crawling around in the dirt. Salamanders were to be found under pieces of wood laying in the shade of a shed. I remember colors, but were there two of them, one eight-ball black and shiny and the other brilliant red or was there only one two toned salamander. In the grove there were grey squirrels jumping through the trees on their way to the corn crib. Crows nested in the grove and behind a shed there was a crabapple tree where a pair of blue birds had a nest. Following behind Dad when he did the spring plowing there were mouse nests to be found and pink hairless baby field mice which I stuck in one of my pockets to be left in the granary.

Probably the biggest threat to my survival on the farm was a family dog that was jealous of me. He would lead me out into the woods then come back to the house alone, refusing to help mom and dad find me. This was on the first farm we rented when I was little more than a toddler. I'm theorizing that being abandoned in the woods by the dog helped me to get used to being alone and perhaps something my mother taught me also helped with that. In teaching me about life she said something like "Life is a stage." Whatever else she told me I took it to mean that we each have parts to play and we are being watched.

I wasn't without playmates on the farm. I had a sister two years younger than I but by the time we left Minnesota my new youngest sister was only a babe-in-arms. There were also neighboring farms within walking distance for a five year old. One of those farms had older kids so I mostly avoided it. The closest farm had a couple of girls near my age and the other one had at least one girl my age and a sibling or two. She had blond hair like my sisters. She was very short and very pretty. When we went back to Minnesota I always hoped we would visit at her home. With only girls to play with on a regular basis I had to wait for the move to California before I learned to enjoy the rough and tumble activities of other little boys.

Before Dad found a home to buy we lived in the trailer we traveled in from Minnesota. In the Willow Pass Trailer Park in Concord, California there were children of all ages and some of them used words unfamiliar to me. Though only six I was long legged and could run and dodge the boys several years older than I was. As I learned to use some of my newly discovered vocabulary on them it was often necessary. Perhaps that's why Mom and Dad sent me to church with a church going family from a nearby trailer. The first church I attended was the Presbyterian Church in Concord. I soon realized that I would have to unlearn some of those new words the older boys had taught me.

Being tall for my age, I found it easy to look upon myself as a protector of my smaller playmates and thought I would become a policeman when I grew up. My poor eyesight put an end to that thought. When I was in the second grade, I recall the class taking a little outing along one of the streets which ran by the school. We were walking single file when a couple of boys started picking on the kid behind me. It was just a little poking and pushing, but he was taking it very badly. I traded places with him and let them poke me instead. I was several inches taller than the rest of the class and the most athletic so they didn't worry me. I ignored them and they soon tired of their antics.

Mom and Dad had high standards for personal behavior so they sent us kids to church. A preacher they considered a hypocrite had pushed them too hard to come to church so they developed a permanent aversion to organized religion. But, they did want me and my sisters to attend Sunday services. The nearest church was a Southern Baptist mission just down the block and around the corner. When I was about ten, I made my profession of faith in Jesus Christ and was baptized. Several years earlier, I had told Jesus in my prayers that I wanted to serve him, and I helped the minister by inviting the neighborhood kids to his youth activities once I was baptized. I was proud to be a Baptist Royal Ambassador as a teenager.

As a saved Christian I understood that "the natural man is an enemy to God". I knew that as a Christian I had the responsibility to choose to follow in the footsteps of Jesus. Making that choice before I had reached the age of puberty, I had little experience with temptation. When I was about twelve and my playmates were big enough to do each other some damage I received a reality check. When we moved to California I had no qualms about wandering alone in the hills between Pacheco and Martinez. Even though I enjoyed being around all sorts of people, I also enjoyed being alone. It was quite a shock to me riding my bicycle alone on the canal road to come across three boys who wanted to fight me. The smallest one was a mean little bully with something to prove. The one nearly my size, but much more muscular was cold. I was not a fighter and had no desire to hurt any of them. Something told me I would be better off letting them take turns punching me in the belly than to put up a fight. I knew that kids could be cruel, but had always figured that most kids think they have an excuse for the bad things they do. I knew that hitting one of them would give them all the excuse they needed to be more than a little cruel. As badly as they hurt me with no provocation, this became a serious reality check for me.

Looking back at that incident I suspect that's probably how the damage was done to my diaphragm (a specialist recently discovered it) for my stamina and athleticism was greatly diminished after that and for me the world was not the friendly place it had been. I lost a lot of self-confidence and occasionally stuttered, but not so often that I received much teasing about it. Diminished self-confidence, stamina, and athleticism likely made it easier for me to follow in the footsteps of Jesus. Pride in physical prowess can lead a young man down a dangerous path of temptation guided by arrogance, thoughts of self importance, and feelings of entitlement. For that reason, I look upon that beating I took as a little extra help from the Lord in keeping me on that narrow path. Thinking of the age of self importance I went through for a short time in my mid-teens, with the advantage of hindsight I am grateful for that extra help from the Lord. I remember seeing product names which were only letters like TCP which was a product for engines, or CVP which stood for Central Valley Project. If there was a letter in it which corresponded with one or more of my initials, I took pleasure in making it about me while I was going through this time of self importance. The reality of my physical shortcomings eventually brought me back down to earth. There are men who have always been outstanding physical specimens who didn't let it go to their heads. I doubt that would have been the case with me.

The Lord opened my eyes to the challenges facing the severely handicapped and with that, reasons to be grateful for what I have. I think it was over the Christmas vacation of my junior year that I came down with a serious strep infection in my sinuses. My mother was monitoring my fever very closely but didn't see any need for a trip to the hospital until I told her my urine had turned wine red. We were told that toxins from the infection had settled in my kidneys resulting in a type of nephrites which I'm not certain how to pronounce or spell. They called it an acute kidney disease at first and sent me home after ten days and the end of the strep infection. They told me I would need complete bed rest until my kidneys had time to heal so I finished my junior year with a home teacher visiting me daily until summer.

The blood and albumin in my urine cleared up sufficiently by the first semester of my senior year that they allowed me to return to school, but now they were calling my kidney disease chronic then latent. All the bed rest I had endured had seriously weakened me, but I went to a regular physical education class at first. Training on the trampoline was first on the schedule and I soon discovered just how weak my legs had become. All it took was one attempt at a front flip: as I came down feet first my legs buckled under me painfully bruising the muscles on the back of my tibia, fibula, and femur.

It was decided that I should attend a semester of what they called modified P.E. instead of the regular class. There I became acquainted with a variety of handicapped kids and pregnant girls. The only classmate I recall was a quadriplegic. He taught me a lot about accepting challenges. He had known what it was to be athletic then lost it all in an accident. It was a privilege for me to give him the help he needed in the boys room when he had to urinate.

During the final semester of my senior year, I met with a Navy recruiter, took some aptitude tests and was looking forward to volunteering and getting some training in electronics while I served my country. The final step that summer was a trip to the Armed Forces Enlistment Center in Oakland where I would take my physical examination. They discovered that my kidney trouble had not completely healed so I was rejected.

By my late teenage years, my enthusiasm for the Baptist Church was waning. They did not believe in dancing and my parents went to parties at the homes of their friends where they square danced. These were good folks who brought their kids with them and I enjoyed sitting around with them watching our parents dance. I began to doubt that God would send all the non-Baptists to hell. There were millions of folks in far off countries who had never heard of Jesus so I began to have some doubts about the Baptist Church.

In a high school, science class in my junior year, I worked hard enough to have a guaranteed "A". The last phase of that class was studying minerals. The teacher had rocks laid out on the lab tables with their names and mineral content listed. We were told to study them in preparation for our last test of the semester. I didn't relish the thought of memorizing all that seemingly useless information while the teacher was just sitting around talking duck hunting with one of my classmates. It just so happened that one of the neatest guys I knew was sitting close by as well as a pretty girl who was a Mormon. Neither Jim nor I knew anything about Mormons so we sat around talking religion with Virginia for several weeks during that science class. I didn't have the slightest idea where she lived and I was too socially backward to think about getting in touch with her during summer vacation. However, my buddy from around the block had joined the Mormon Church so I started talking to him about religion. To my surprise he was just as full of answers to questions my Baptist Minister couldn't answer as that young lady in my science class had been.

As my circle of Mormon friends widened I began to feel so much at home with them that I accepted an invitation to be taught by a pair of their local part-time missionaries. The gospel they taught made as much sense to me as the answers to my questions from Mormon friends so I took the missionary lessons already feeling like one of them. Here was a person who didn't believe that the rest of the world was going to hell. The confidence in the Lord which I had lost was restored and the world was suddenly a better place. I had lost my self confidence, but it returned. I was a new person as I became a member of a church with a perfect organization, or so they told me.

Being in my late teens I felt quite independent of my parents and sisters. It was very easy for me to feel like I had been adopted by a lovely family in Martinez Ward. Gordon and Doreen Barney had a son a couple of years younger than I and two daughters to replace my own sisters. Doreen's mother and father, the Hipwells, lived next door to them and soon I was calling them Nanny and Poppy. Sunday dinner at the Hipwells with the Barneys also in attendance became the usual thing.

After joining the LDS Church, I finally started dating and eventually found a steady date in the person of a lovely young lady who moved an hour or two away after a few months. Some say "Distance makes the heart grow fonder", while others say "distance makes the heart go wander". The latter was true for both of us. I wasn't dating after she moved away, but I did attend the dances for the Mormon youth. At the last dance I would attend before leaving on my mission I had one dance with Sylvia (the young lady I would eventually marry). I was completely captivated. We had just one date after that and that was for some bowling and time to talk. It was reassuring to discover we were both quite taken with each other. This development was going to make two years in the mission field seem longer.

Preparing for a mission in less than two years required diligent efforts in studying my new-found religion. The church has Institutes of Religion for college kids where there is the need, but whether or not there was such a thing close by I was invited to attend the Seminary class with the high school kids and jumped at the chance. High school kids attended seminary before school started at Alhambra Union High School. That meant getting up a couple of hours early and attending the class at the Martinez Ward building then catching a ride to work at the SF-Oakland Bay Bridge Toll Plaza where I worked in the stock room as a junior clerk.

After becoming a member of the Church it didn't take long for the Bishop to find a couple of church callings for me. Soon I was involved in the youth program of the Church as the secretary of the Young Men's Mutual Improvement Association, meeting every Wednesday evening for instruction and activities, some of them co-educational as the Young Women's MIA also met on Wednesday evenings. My second responsibility was with the young men's priesthood activities. The General secretary of the Aaronic Priesthood was a very busy family man from Utah who was serving his residency at the county hospital there in Martinez. The demands of his residency left him in need of an assistant for his church responsibilities and that was to be me. He was well endowed with charisma, he had a lovely wife, and some small children. He was a natural to be my mentor in family and priesthood responsibilities.

Working full time and being active in the church meant it was already a busy time for me, then I joined the Martinez Ward Basket Ball Team. I was a bit awkward, but my 6'6" height made me a valuable player. The other members of the team were such excellent players that we became the regional champs and got to go to the All Church Playoffs in Provo, Utah at Brigham Young University. The decisive game in our local regional playoffs was played after I received the worst sprained ankle; it had ever been my misfortune to experience. The top and sides of my foot were black and blue from the base of my toes to well above my ankle. My mentor taped it up for me and I hobbled around the court trying to guard a taller center on the team from our U.C. Berkeley Institute of Religion. Their center was at least a couple of inches taller than I and slender and more nimble than I even when I wasn't suffering from a sprained ankle, so he became even more of a threat because he didn't feel the need to guard me closely. Somehow I found myself with the ball before I had time to get near the basket.

WILL THE REAL MORMONS STAND UP AND SOUND THE ALARM?

With my bum ankle I couldn't attempt a jump shot so while standing flatfooted I sent the ball flying high into the rafters beyond his reach. To everyone's astonishment, including mine, the ball went through the hoop with nothing but net. After that their center had to play me more closely which made him less of a threat.

With all these things behind me, after little more than a year and one half I had saved only about half of what I would need to support myself for two years in the mission field. The Bishop or was it the stake president who felt I was ready. Someone convinced the Stake High Priest's Quorum to make up the difference.

Because of the opportunities I took advantage of for study and Church callings, within a year of my baptism I had spoken at a stake conference in front of a crowd of about 2,200 Latter-Day Saints. Less than a year after that I was serving as a full time missionary in the Southern States Mission which covered Georgia, Alabama, and South Carolina, but not with the same enthusiasm or reverence for my leaders which I had when I spoke at the Stake Conference. Before leaving on my mission I had faced another reality check, this one involving my local Church leaders instead of a confrontation with thugs on the canal road.

By the time my mentor had finished his residency and moved on, I was prepared to take over as Acting General secretary of the Aaronic Priesthood and I was still the Secretary of the YMMIA. Both callings required me to keep attendance records of the young men, and they needed to be accurate as attendance at priesthood meetings and YMMIA figured in the eligibility for priesthood awards handed out yearly.

Attendance records were pretty simple, but with one complication; when a member of the Aaronic Priesthood attended YMMIA in one of the other wards I had to count it as though he had attended our ward's YMMIA. I asked them to tell me when they had attended YMMIA in another ward so I could count them on the attendance rolls, but I told them if they left the other ward early and showed up in Martinez Ward having already missed most of the meeting here, they would not be counted in attendance. Sure enough, one of them came in to YMMIA near the end of the meeting at a time when missing two more meetings would mean he couldn't qualify for his Aaronic Priesthood Award. I informed him that if he missed one more time he wouldn't receive his award. I informed the Bishop also and it was up to the him to inform the boy's father that his son was in danger of failing to qualify for the award.

In the remaining weeks before award time, the young man missed another meeting. When it came time for the awards to be given out I was in attendance. I couldn't believe it, the young man who had missed too many meetings was called up with the others to receive his award. No one had told me that I had goofed on my record keeping I so stood up and told the Bishop that the young man in question didn't qualify for the award because of too many missed meetings. I was called into the Bishop's office along with the boy, his father, and the Bishop. The father wanted to know why he hadn't been notified when his son still had one more meeting to miss before becoming ineligible. The Bishop pointed at me and said no one had told him. I politely objected, but it did no good. He received his award and it was announced from the podium that I had failed to keep proper records. Except for the lack of bruises I felt just like three guys had jumped me and beat the crap out of me again.

The father felt he had to stick up for his son, but why would the Bishop conspire against me? What-ever-the-case, he had decided to ignore the attendance records I was in charge of without getting my side of the story. It would be many years before I would have enough confidence in my leaders to confide in them.

Before leaving on my mission, I had the opportunity to be interviewed by an Apostle who happened to be in the area. I didn't hold anything back from him except for that confrontation with the Bishop. I just did not have any confidence that it would do any good. After what the Apostle said to me I certainly didn't want to get caught in a showdown between my Bishop, the boy's father, and that Apostle. It gave me cause to wonder what kind of God our leaders worshiped. I wanted to go on a mission and didn't want to take any chances on being prevented from going because of a blowup with a Bishop and someone who obviously did not have my best interest at heart. My friends had told me that though the Church was perfect, the people were not. Something was wrong in the Church, but I wasn't ready to deal with it so I pushed my concerns aside to be faced at a later time. My conversion made such a big change in my live that serving the Lord as a full time missionary was my highest priority.

Although I wasn't emotionally or socially mature enough to confront the Bishop again, I did complain to a lot of members of the ward hoping that my complaints might reach the Bishop and elicit a reaction from him. It didn't and I'm afraid I became too used to complaining. For all the complaining I did, no one suggested that I confront them or take them before the Stake High Council and I was too new in the Church to realize I had that option. They owed me an apology and I knew it wasn't right that they should get away with behavior which could cost them their eternal souls. Lying and making false accusations are the Lord's favorite reasons for sending unrepentant sinners to hell and I was concerned about them.

CHAPTER 8

MY MISSION

On Saturday, March 19th, 1961 my best friends, the Gordon Barney family, dropped me off at the Oakland Greyhound Bus terminal to catch the 12:15 P.M. bus to Salt Lake City. Because of all the stops the bus makes it took about 19 hours to make the trip. Arriving in Salt Lake City at 7:00 A.M. I ate breakfast, cleaned up and caught the 9:00 A.M. Greyhound to Provo where I attended Sunday School with a young lady from Martinez Ward, and her roommates. They prepared a nice hot lunch and then a young man also from Martinez Ward, came over for a visit. He saw me down to the bus depot where I caught the 3:15 Greyhound for SLC where Brother and Sister Eddie Isaacson picked me up and took me to their home for supper. They visited with me until 9:00 P.M. when they dropped me off at the Mission Home.

I spent a week in the Mission Home at 31 North State Street with perhaps a couple of hundred Missionaries, eight of us in the room where I slept. We ate at the nearby Hotel Utah using the ten dollar meal ticket we each had obtained to cover our needs for the week. An LDS colored man who helped serve us bore his testimony to the group; I was impressed.

The instruction we received was very helpful. In addition to instruction and practice at greeting and teaching potential investigators, we were given practical tips on ironing and mending our clothes, personal hygiene, preparing meals, etc. Saturday and Sunday we were on our own. Saturday I walked 13 blocks to visit Afton Hipwell's brother-in-law at his barbershop. I had Sunday dinner in the Garth Naylor home. Garth had served in the mission field with Gordon Barney, my good friend's father. Garth was out of town so I missed meeting that well known restaurateur and joint owner of Farmington's Heidelberg Restaurant. Afton Hipwell, the grandmother of my good friend, Rich Barney, had arranged the visit. Garth had served his mission in California and Afton Hipwell was a favorite of the missionaries because of the wonderful meals she served as well as the free laundry service she provided for them. Sunday night I enjoyed cake and ice cream at the home of a Bishop whose son Gary was one of my roommates. The Elder's girl friend knitted me a pair of slippers to take with me to the Southern states Mission. I enjoyed their use for quite a few years.

Near the end of our stay in the Mission Home we had a bit of a surprise. One of our roommates wasn't going to complete his mission. It seems that he and his girl friend had decided to get married thinking if they did it secretly he could still serve his mission. The secret was discovered.

Monday morning, March 26th a bunch of us left Salt Lake City in a first class railcar, a plush Vista Dome car on the D & RG Railroad. Our car was switched to a different train in Pueblo, Colorado until we reached St. Louis. There we had to depart the Vista Dome and board what in comparison seemed like a converted cattle car as we headed for Atlanta. Most of the way to Atlanta there were 19 new missionaries to attempt turning the other occupants of the car to Mormonism. Eventually I had a turn chatting up a couple of teenage girls who were traveling together. I had been given an ample supply of business cards with the Southern States Mission Home address on them. Several times during my mission I received letters from one of the girls, Molly, and eventually one of the letters told of her conversion and baptism. I would visit her at BYU on my way home.

Thursday, March 29th at 10:00 A.M. we arrived in Atlanta and made the short trip to the Mission Home in Decatur where I stayed until time to catch the midnight Greyhound to Ozark, Alabama. In

Ozark I was met by my first senior companion. He was short and my 6' 6" height gave us a Mutt and Jeff appearance. Back in those innocent days, we often had to share a regular full sized bed so having a small companion was a blessing.

I experienced a bit of culture shock at seeing blacks ride in the back of the bus. Then there was also the fact of two drinking fountains, one for colored people and the other for whites. Three separate bathrooms, male, female, and colored were also a surprise. Being in Georgia and Alabama between March of 61 and late March of 63 meant that I was only a few hours away from some of the historical civil rights disturbances of that era.

I would end up spending nine months in this first area which ran eighty miles from Eufaula, Alabama near the Georgia border to Enterprise, Alabama near Fort Rucker. Covering such a large area had made it difficult to keep up with our study schedule. We were to get up at 6:00 A.M., study for an hour, shower, eat breakfast and be out and about by eight or nine, I'm not certain which. If we were an hour's drive from the apartment when we finished with our last meeting it was difficult to get home in time for an hour of study and in bed by ten. Fortunately, the area was split after three months and my companion went to Eufaula to be joined by another Elder, while I receive a new companion in Ozark.

Mondays were what we called diversion day, "D" day for short. We washed clothes, went shopping after planning our weekly needs for food, then perhaps went to a movie or got together for sports if there were enough other Elders nearby, but there was not near our area. Mondays were also the day we wrote letters to friends and family. Though I only had one date with Sylvia, now my wife, we were both quite smitten, so we exchanged romantic letters. Fortunately she didn't write very often because of her class schedule which made it easier to keep my mind on missionary work, she was commuting from Concord to San Francisco State College or University. I remember a missionary who received tapes from his sweetheart which he listened to on "D" day. It took several days for him to recover from one of those tapes.

Fort Rucker had a chapel which LDS military members had an assigned time to use. Some of the military members also attended the little brick chapel about half way to Eufaula. The Branch President and his first councilor were with the military and were from the west. They attended meetings on the base and out in the country with the local members. This meant driving about one hundred miles per Sunday.

While one of the military men was in the hospital we would occasionally drop by to check on his family. Mid-morning one day when his wife finally came to the door it was apparent she had been sleeping. She said that she had started sleeping in the day time because of the cockroaches. At night their cat, Meesh, kept her awake jumping around on the bed. Meesh, with her night vision and sharp hearing knew the cockroaches were crawling around on the ceiling. When she turned on the light to see why Meesh was jumping around, she noticed that Meesh was looking up at the ceiling. The sight of a ceiling full of cockroaches put her into near panic mode. With the lights on the cockroaches kept out of sight so she stayed awake most of the night and slept most of the day. Hey, those roaches were three inches long.

Fort Rucker was the rotary wing and fixed wing training headquarters for the Army which drew people from all across the country, but most of the Latter-Day-Saints were from Utah. Also living in Ozark was a civilian flight instructor from Holland. He lived in Ozark with his wife and four children with another on the way. Their children included a pretty little blond three year old. Serving on a mission is about doing the Lord's work, but personal growth is accelerated. My fatherly feelings for the three year old told me that I was ready to have children of my own. When Sylvia and I married, two of our children were girls and they turned out to be every bit as cute as that lovely child. But, when it comes to your own children, your love for them does not depend upon cuteness.

The brick chapel which was home to the little branch of the Church was on property donated by Brother David Hartzog. The Hartzogs had a married son nearby, and three lovely daughters at home. They were always on their best behavior around us. A quick, short handshake was the closest thing to intimacy allowed between a missionary and any female younger than our mothers.

Getting directions from Brother Hartzog was confusing at first. If he told us to turn right past the branch, was he referring to the chapel, a creek, or a fork in the road? The biggest difficulty was when directions depended on the color of a house. I had never seen a black house, but they usually figured in verbal directions. The houses were all white or nearly bare wood, but the color referred to the people inside the house. I had no idea how to tell the difference between a black sharecropper's house and a white sharecropper's house if no one was sitting on the porch or no kids playing in the yard. I wondered if that meant that a white sharecropper had the same standing in the community as a black sharecropper. Having eaten by the dim light of a kerosene lamp in a sharecropper's home, I sometimes wonder if I have eaten jack rabbit or perhaps something more unusual for supper.

Door to door tracting was nearly always the last choice when it came to proselyting so we preferred to look up the members and obtain referrals from them. We were given some interesting local history by old timers we came across. One old timer remembered back in the late 1800s being in a meeting while the KKK was galloping their horses around the meeting place firing their guns in order to disrupt the meeting and possibly scare some of the hated Mormons off.

One day, we stopped to visit a retired school teacher living out in the country. What an interesting visit. She spoke of a place nearby where a group of the Shakers had lived. The group died out because they didn't believe in having babies. She seemed pretty old to me, but her mind was alert and full of interesting information. She won me over when she looked at our foreheads and announced that I was more intelligent than my companion. I thought my compassion was a sharp missionary, but being the junior companion, it gave me a little satisfaction to hear her elevate me above him.

One spring morning we happened upon the home and small acreage of the widow Carol. Sister Alma Carol's major responsibility was taking care of her aged mother. It was early in the year and none of her kinfolk had come around to work up her garden yet so we assumed the task. She had a small plow for that job. It was small enough so that one of us could pull and the other could pull down and push on the handles, like wheel barrow handles. The garden area was full of very loose sandy loam or we would have needed a horse to do the pulling. It was a good feeling to have helped them.

Organizing a softball tournament was as popular with us missionaries as it was with the kids. It improved the status of the LDS kids and gave us the opportunity to become acquainted with non-member kids and their parents. Ice cream socials were also a favorite, with homemade ice cream. The first time we had one in Eufaula, perhaps at the home of sister Lillie Carol, we had borrowed several hand-crank ice cream makers and wouldn't you know it; the one I was cranking didn't have a dasher in it. I should have known better, but I cranked until the party was nearly over before I took it apart to check on the dasher.

We didn't have the success some missionaries enjoyed in baptizing kids, but we did teach and baptize five adults plus we taught a few whom members or our supervising elders baptized.

Our most outstanding contacts were discovered while tracting. The family consisted of husband, wife, and son. The lady of the house was a heavy smoker and when she borrowed my brand new triple combination, it fell open to the word of wisdom. When she first saw us near her home, she saw a glow around us which sometimes occurs around people with whom she is going to have a special bond. In one of our meetings with the family, she reported having a dream wherein the Devil took on the form of her minister and was riding in a fire red Dodge Lancer having "The True Word of God" written on it. Her husband also had an interesting manifestation while visiting relatives on a genealogy gathering quest. She said he took on the persona of his father which gained them favor in the eyes of relatives from whom they expected little or no cooperation.

One weekend I had the feeling that we should stop and pay them a visit, but my companion wouldn't go for it. When we did drop by, they were in terrible shape. They had been up all night talking religion with a minister, drinking coffee in order to stay awake. She also had returned to her habit of heavy smoking. She had gone from two cigarettes per day to once again smoking like a fiend. She decided that since the Word of Wisdom had been only a suggestion at first then later became a commandment, she didn't need to feel guilty. In her sleep deprived mind she had some things I had told her about blacks and the priesthood twisted around and I was being blamed for her confused state of mind.

Needless to say I was extremely disappointed. My leaders were concerned about me and wondered what they could do for me. Remembering what a negative influence my Bishop had been, I wasn't ready to open up to the Mission President. Eventually I asked for a transfer. Nine months was a long time for a missionary to stay in one area. I had developed some good memories there. I was transferred to Augusta, Georgia on the 31st of December, 1961.

My first month in Augusta my companion was an Elder who had been there for several months. I hated to see him transferred after only one month. My next companion stayed with me for the final two months of his mission. While they figured out what to do about a missionary without a companion one of the supervising Elders stayed with me the remaining couple of weeks of my time in Augusta.

My three months in Augusta had been busy and productive. We taught ten people whom we or local members baptized and confirmed members of the church. The first young couple we baptized gained strong testimonies and have witnessed the power of prayer. A widow and her son were ready for the gospel. We administered to her when she was sick and left some pamphlets. A week or two later she unexpectedly showed up at a group meeting and testified to the truthfulness of the gospel and bore witness that the Lord had helped her overcome her desire to smoke.

We became especially close to a part-member family. The wife has been working hard to get her husband into the church for the three or four years they have been married. One Saturday morning, he was taking us fishing. It was a foggy morning and my companion was driving his personal vehicle, a Renault Dauphine. Bobby must have been lost, and we certainly didn't have the slightest idea where we were. Then suddenly we were going downhill and there was a cement wall in front of us. The pavement had a thin layer of wet sand on it and when my companion put on the brakes the Renault seemed to pick up speed. The front end of the car was totaled and my forehead broke the windshield as my knee put a big dent in the dash. They wanted me to be looked at by a physician, but I wouldn't hear of it. I was very lucky for I must have had at least a slight concussion. For several days, perhaps weeks, I felt fuzzy headed and a little distant.

Bobby felt so bad about the car that he insisted on repairing it. He was a highly skilled welder at the nearby Redstone Missile plant. At his suggestion, we checked with the local salvage yards until we found a suitable Renault which had the rear end totaled, but an excellent front end. Bobby cut the front ends off with a torch and welded the good front end from the other Renault onto the good part of my companion's vehicle. I worked on the dashboards and took off the fenders while my companion assisted Bobby with the welding.

An episode showing the sometimes high pressure atmosphere in the mission field occurred in connection with a family we were working with and our supervising Elders. The Elders were practicing their positive attitudes on the sister by pressuring her to feed them lunch. All she had available was something she had planned on using to fix supper for her family when her husband got home so they ate her husband's supper for lunch. With the sister in tears the Relief Society President was soon involved, then the Mission President. We found out a day or two later. Before the week was out our supervising Elders, the perpetrators, stopped by to warn us against pressuring the members to feed us. Quite innocently, I asked what that was about. The senior companion of the two said that some Elders had pressured a sister to feed them her husband's supper. Again quite innocently, I said, "Gee, Elder, I can't think of anyone who would do something like that." The senior companion took on a steely pose while his companion simply hung his head in shame. I felt proud of the Elder who was ashamed.

On April 2nd my supervising elder met us at the small house we rented and told me I had 20 minutes to catch the Greyhound to Phoenix City, Alabama. The Phoenix City Alabama/Columbus Georgia District was in flux so my companion would be with me for only the following month. He and his previous companion had been very busy so I soon had the privilege of taking part in the baptizing or confirming of three investigators. I parted company with him and was given a brand new Elder for a few weeks. We didn't have a car so we spent three weeks solid doing door to door tracting on foot. It wasn't my favorite pastime so I was glad to be transferred to an established area across the river in Phoenix City, Alabama where I would be stationed with my permanent companion for my stay in Phoenix City. We made an imposing pair as he was about 6' 6" the same as I.

Our three months together were very busy. We baptized and confirmed four of our investigators. I baptized one of them in Lake Oliver. Today the Bishops have a youth committee, but back then in the Southern States Mission or at least the Phoenix City/Columbus District it was the Missionary Youth Committee and we were in charge of one. They wanted activities for the summer while school was out so we organized Saturday morning car washes and donut sales. My companion and I drove to Atlanta in the wee hours of Saturday morning and picked up a car load of Flakey Kreme or Krispy Kreme donuts, I don't recall which. We had taken out the back seat so we could put more there and filled up the trunk also, then drove them back to Phoenix City/Columbus by 8:00 A.M. and sold them door to door with the help of the youth. While we built up our funds for a big summer bash, the ward had a party or two. Their ice cream socials included homemade ice cream and homemade A&W Root Beer. They purchased some A&W syrup, some dry ice, added water in a ten or fifteen gallon pot, then let it bubble until it was cold enough and well carbonated. Making root beer floats with homemade ice cream created a wonderful treat.

The "end of summer vacation" party was the one we did up right. We went to a meat packing plant and purchased half a hog with funds from donut sales. A park out in tall timber had been reserved for our luau style hog roast. With nearly a dozen missionaries in the district it didn't take long to dig a deep pit, place a lot of fire wood in it and some cobble stones on top. When the firewood had finished burning and the rocks were good and hot we wrapped the half a hog in chicken wire after wrapping it in gunny sack and banana leaves, then tossed it onto the rocks, dumped some water on it, and left it covered with dirt for several hours. Wow, the best roast pork I've eaten.

But, all was not well in the Phoenix City/Columbus District. One of the Missionaries and his companion, a pair from Columbus, was spending a lot of time at the home of a teenage girl in our area who was on our Missionary Youth Committee. Someone volunteered the information that said Missionary had taken the 14 year old bowling for her birthday. I knew that this could be bad for morale so I reported it to my Supervising Elder. He told me that he would deal with it and I was not to get involved any further. He said if Elder Franklin D, Richards found out he would come and clean house because there had already been too many problems with Missionaries. One of his missionaries had gone home early and he did not want the scrutiny another problem in his district might bring.

I hadn't had any problem keeping my mind off the southern belles, but in Phoenix City, we had a Missionary Youth Committee to meet with quite often. One of the young ladies on the committee was just a little younger than my baby sister which helped me to feel at home there. But, there was a young lady who was a little older named Gwen who was also on the committee. She had demonstrated her respect for my need to remain aloof, for missionaries could not date, hold hands with, or be alone with a girl. One evening when leaving the recreation hall at the close of an activity as I entered the long hallway, empty except for her and I on the way out of the building, she came out the same way about twenty feet behind me. I didn't slow down and she didn't speed up. It would have been awkward for me if we had walked out together because she was becoming a distraction for me.

I'm not certain how to describe my feelings for Gwen; extreme admiration and fondness for certain, but I thought she was the prettiest girl in three states. Just thinking that she was the prettiest girl in three states makes me wonder if she was really that pretty or if I was that captivated by her. It became obvious to me one Sunday at Sacrament Meeting that I had to take action to prevent her from becoming even more of a distraction. Gwen was sitting up in the choir seats and I couldn't take my eyes off her. Afterwards she coyly accused me of staring at her during the meeting. I was too busy blushing and being embarrassed to realize that she must have been looking at me. I couldn't take any chances on my feelings for her becoming strong enough to pose a problem so I asked my Supervising Elder for a transfer. On August 13th an Elder who had his own vehicle was being transferred the same day as I was so he dropped me off in my next area of labor, Austell, Georgia.

My first companion in Austell was my companion for less than a month before it was time for him to transfer. They rarely transfer both Elders out at the same time so that someone who knows the area will be around for awhile to help the new Elder get acquainted. He knew his duty and proceeded to make the rounds introducing me to all of his contacts. I'll never forget an elderly sister he took me to meet. A colored servant met us at the door. As soon as we were brought to the setting room to visit the lady of the house, my companion took out a Lincoln head cent and flipped it at her. Before the maid had left the room the lady of the house began her tirade. It appeared to be a well rehearsed speech about what a terrible villain Lincoln was for releasing those slaves, and she didn't merely call them slaves. It was with mixed feelings that I listened to the embarrassing bit of vitriol which seemed to last much too long. I was too stunned to be able to tell you which source of embarrassment was the strongest. I was embarrassed for the sister for saying it, for the servant for having to listen to it, and I was embarrassed for the Church for having doctrine which enabled the sister to feel justified in speaking up so frankly.

I don't recall which area I was in when I met a member of the ward or branch in which I was serving who had an interesting story to tell. She was five to fifteen years my senior, perhaps more. She was in the French Mission when a bunch of missionaries became polygamists. I don't recall the Elder's name, but he was a full time missionary who was an assistant to the Mission President. He pulled the wool over the eyes of some of his fellow missionaries and they came back to the USA and organized a polygamous group. Because he was a member of the mission presidency, he had some freedom of movement. He would drive around and find some landmark, then tell some missionaries that he had a vision instructing them go to this place near the landmark and they would find someone ready to be taught the gospel. He gave them the kind of instructions which made success somewhat likely. If they didn't find someone to teach it was their lack of faith.

All the members were very nice to us. One of them had a seventeen year old daughter, a lovely girl. They invited us to go on an outing with them one day. I don't remember the seating arrangements, but there was no hand-holding. In a heavily wooded area they pulled off the road so that the brother could introduce us to something he called muscadines. They grew singly on a vine which somehow managed to reach the branches of a large tree. They were at least an inch in diameter with very thick black or dark blue skins and flesh much like a concord grape in taste and texture. We also stopped at an orchard and bought some golden delicious apples. I haven't tasted better, but I eventually did manage to obtain a bare root tree several feet tall which I planted in my back yard in Elk Grove, California. It was like having a bit of northern Georgia in my back yard when it matured enough to bear fruit.

My new companion arrived on September 8th. He stayed with me for three and one half months. We baptized six of our investigators there including a young couple who referred us to the wife's younger brothers. After their baptism, one of the boys arranged for us to talk to his class at the public school he attended, which was a first for me. The mother of the two boys we baptized as most southerners was quite willing to feed us more often than we thought prudent, but we did eat supper with them at least once. Cornbread made with course cornmeal, black eyed peas with fatback, and fried okra; good eating!

The non-member mother of the two boys we baptized was scheduled for brain surgery and asked for a blessing from us. I suspect that her daughter and son-in-law whom we had baptized, encouraged her to ask for the blessing. The surgeon was expecting a difficult time in removing a very large tumor. It turned out to be small and the surgery went well. We were grateful for the Lords intervention and perhaps a little surprised for we didn't experience any special feelings about the blessing we gave her.

There were enough members in the Marietta area for a ward with an active youth program. One day our supervising Elders insisted we attend MIA. The program included a kickoff for the back to school season. Part of the program included a song sang to the tune of the Double Mint Gum song and a pretty little thirteen year old girl who had a crush on me, apparently, and wanted to sing it as a duet with me. I love to sing in the choir, but had never sang a solo or duet in front of a crowd so I was quite embarrassed.

Brother and sister McKinney were a lovely young couple who were very good to us. We were in Austell during the big freeze of 1962. The temperature went down to 4 degrees above zero along with an ice storm. Tree branches were hanging low with ice and plumbing froze up all over. It lasted at least a couple of weeks. Fortunately the McKinneys took pity on us and had us stay with them because there was ice in our bathtub. We took sister McKinney's father to visit a friend at a nearby asylum for the mentally disturbed. That was an eye opener!

The Cuban missile crisis occurred while we were in Austell and since we were in range of those missiles there were a lot of nervous folks in that area. Dobbins Air Force Base was nearby which made us wonder if we might be a target should things go wrong.

There wasn't much happening in our area, so the Supervising Elders wanted us to waylay kids on their way home from school. That didn't sound like something we ought to be doing. Our supervising Elder's area took in Marietta and most of the members in the Ward. We had a few members in our area, mostly out in the country and a couple of tiny towns. With the advantage of hindsight I have to admit that this area was more like my first area in Alabama, but smaller. However, my last area in Phoenix City, Alabama was very busy while in Austell we didn't have any responsibility for a youth committee or enough going on to distract me from homesickness.

The stress of missionary work, not having any investigators, and feeling that I was out of tune with the program was affecting my digestion. I believe I was developing an ulcer judging by the painful stomach gas pressure and belching I was experiencing. Nearly time for supper, we stopped at a member's home on the way back to our apartment. She volunteered to fix me a sandwich when my belching made her aware of my hunger pangs. It was a tomato and lettuce sandwich with plenty of black pepper. The poor sister felt really bad because I began belching all the more loudly, non-stop. It was a painful ordeal. I had to keep cabbage on hand so I could chew it up and swallow the juice. A family friend had told me of the benefits of raw cabbage juice for an ulcer.

My spirits were low enough so that when my companion was transferred out, it only took a week for me to decide to tell the Supervising Elders that I wanted to go home. Instead I was transferred to the Mission Home in Decatur. I spent two weeks there, then they transferred me to Charleston, South Carolina for my last six weeks where an Elder was waiting for a companion. They gave me two weeks to become acquainted with the area before they shipped him out and sent me a young, brand new Elder to train. He arrived about the same time I received a "Dear John" letter from Sylvia.

My two year stint as a missionary was up in about four weeks, so we didn't accomplish much though I did my best to keep him busy. Charleston was a beautiful city and I'm glad I was able to spend some time there before being released from my mission. We spent some time around the scenic park by the bay asking the Golden Questions, "How much do you know about the Mormon Church and would you like to know more?" One little old Presbyterian lady had an unusual reply to those questions. She said, "I know you Mormons are racist bigots", then she proceeded to read us the riot act.

I was in Charleston just long enough to get caught up the local disrespect for leaders which was growing there. The Mission hierarchy was playing mind-games with the Supervising Elders again. They were told to tell the Elders they supervised to "Do as we do". Even though the other Missionaries in the District were doing better than they were. When we had a District meeting they finished by saying "Do as we do, Elders". Then, of course whenever we saw another pair of Missionaries driving around town we reached out the window and formed a hook with the index finger as we shouted "Hang it in your ear Elder". That, I suppose, is exactly what we were expected to do in order to embarrass them.

March 23rd, I caught the 8:00 A.M. Greyhound from Charleston to Austell, Georgia where I met my good buddy Merle Hult. He had been in North Carolina dropping a friend of his off after driving him all the way from California. Merle had served his mission in Japan and when one of his former missionary companions was released, Merle drove him to his home in North Carolina. We went to the Ponders to spend the night. The next morning we picked up the Pepper boys and took them to Sunday School and Sacrament Meeting at Marietta Ward. It was disappointing to discover that rumors had started up suggesting that I had transferred out of Austell because I had been dating an unmarried sister of the Pepper boys.

After eating at Peppers we went to the Mission Home to pick up my travel money then headed for Phoenix City, Alabama. We stopped at the home of some members where Gwen had lived while I was serving in that area. To my great surprise and disappointment, I didn't get to see Gwen because she had moved to Bountiful, Utah to live with the mother and sister of one of the Elders who had been assigned to Phoenix City for awhile. I don't remember the Elder's name, but I was told by someone, if not the Elder himself that I was invited to stop and visit at his home on my way back to California.

We took turns driving by trading off every two hours. The one who wasn't driving could relax as needed or nap while the other drove. We stopped in Davenport, Iowa to visit my childhood friends, the Harry Crooks from Pacheco, California. While there we took the short trip to Carthage Jail where Joseph Smith was martyred. On the way home, we went by way of Liberty Jail where the prophet was incarcerated for several months. The church was in the process of building a visitor's center around it so we didn't get to see more than the outside of it. We also stopped in Independence, Missouri to see the temple site which was split into three plots, one owned by our church, one by the RLDS Church, and the other by the Church of Christ Temple Lot sometimes called the Hedrikites (sp?).

The day before we were to reach the Salt Lake City area, we called the mother of the Missionary who had sent Gwen to live with her. We arrived there on a Thursday evening when Gwen and the Missionary's sister were getting ready to go to a party. Gwen hardly noticed me as she and the other young lady left the room whispering excitedly together as they anticipated the evening they were preparing for. It was good to see her so happy, but then she always seemed happy. In my state of diminished self-confidence it didn't seem likely that they could have been whispering about me. It had only been a few weeks since Sylvia had sent me a Dear John letter so I was still a little numb from that. I failed to even try to arrange for some time with her and discover what kind of feelings she might have had for me. Besides, it seemed likely that she had feelings for the Elder who had arranged for her to stay with his mother and sister. This left me with no closure for my obsession with her. At a time in our marriage when Sylvia and I were not getting along so well I had a dream which gave me the closure I needed. In the dream I was in the presence of a being or beings who non-verbally made me feel comforted about having married Sylvia instead of Gwen.

The closure did not put an end to my concern for her. Down through the years I would occasionally wonder about Gwen and hope she had been as lucky in finding true love as had I with Sylvia.

The next day we went to Provo where Merle and I parted company temporarily. I went to visit Molly, the young lady whom I had talked to on the train headed for Atlanta some two years earlier. She was all excited about a quiz in some magazine which was supposed to reveal our readiness for marriage. If she was checking me out as a potential marriage partner it didn't take long for her to find out that I wasn't interested. I was too brokenhearted because of the "Dear John" letter from Sylvia and the short glimpse of Gwen ignoring me to consider how to let her down easy.

After my lunch with Molly I met up with one of my favorite companions and went home with him to Preston, Idaho. On Saturday we harrowed a field of potatoes or prepared the field for planting, then double dated with his sweetheart and her best friend. I held hands with my date for awhile but she wasn't interested in me and I was still broken up over Sylvia and Gwen so the evening must have been a big dud for her. I watched Conference on Sunday with the family of my former companion.

Sometime during my stay in Utah, I made contact with the doctor who had been my mentor in church responsibilities when I was a recent convert. When I mentioned that I was considering becoming a chiropractor - wow! Scratch one mentor! What a disappointing month!! A "Dear John" from Sylvia, Gwen ignored me, and my mentor was really upset at me. On top of that I had probably ruined Molly's day by trampling all over her expectations.

On Monday, my former companion drove me back down to BYU where I met up with Merle again and we resumed our trip home. I admire Merle a great deal and the trip had been a good time for me to receive some counsel from him.

CHAPTER 9

GETTING ON WITH MY LIFE

Now that I had completed my mission, there was still the unfinished business of how to deal with inconsistencies surrounding my backstabbing Bishop. I had swallowed the Kool-Aid; "God will not allow your prophet to lead you astray, never say 'No' to your leaders, your Bishop is a prophet to the ward you live in, you are a prophet to those whom you preside over, we are obligated to sustain our leaders unless we know they are guilty of serious sin." Being a liar and a false accuser placed one in the category of those who are highly favored to be sent to hell. And yet, no one would dare suggest I should do something about a Bishop whom I accused of being a lying back stabber. There was something wrong, but I was not ready to face up to what the implications might be. It was sapping my spiritual strength and hurting my relationship with the Lord. Over the following years, I would from time to time hear evidence of the power Bishops had in the Church. In some places reading the wrong book could get a member disfellowshipped or excommunicated.

I have to admit that my Bishop was watching out for me. The first thing he did was to inquire about my finances. I told him I needed a couple of tires for my car so that I could look for a job. He arranged for that and asked in return that I so some service work in order to reimburse the church. Canning season was a ways off so in the meantime he sent me to help out at girls camp. It was tough duty, up early in the morning to catch some trout to share with a leader or two, then help with the fire wood for the evening outdoor fireside program. And yes, I was still a big kid who liked to place firecrackers in the logs for the bonfire. I was not disappointed in the volume and duration of the screams emitted by the girls for the "bang" of the firecracker came at the perfect time as the girls sang about the bunny asking for help, "or the hunter will shoot me dead". The "bang" of the firecracker and the singing of the word "shoot" came simultaneously. Later in the summer there would be less enjoyable duty taking a hoe to the weeds on a Church owned farm.

I had been home only a week or two when Stan Dahlin from Concord Ward called me up and invited me to go on a picnic with the Sunday School Class he taught. He was a favorite with the youth and I knew who he was. He was Sylvia's Sunday School teacher. Sylvia was highly impressed with Stan and Valentine Dahlin. Sylvia showed up at the picnic so it became apparent that Brother Dahlin had invited me at her request or at least for her benefit as she had broken up with her new sweetheart. The world was a better place once more. We would be sealed in the Los Angeles Temple in less than a year. The Dahlins accompanied us to Los Angeles and we had a second couple to help enlarge the small wedding party in the persons of a couple, Jon and Diane, who had been at Fort Rucker while I was serving on my mission and living nearby in Ozark, Alabama. Both couples were dear to us and their presence increased the joy of that special day.

Sylvia was nearly finished at San Francisco State when I popped the question, but she had been saving for a semester at Brigham Young University so we set the date for the following March. Our marriage started off very well and fifteen years later some folks thought we were still newly-weds.

We decided I should continue my education, so while Sylvia had a very good job, I took a part-time job and went to a nearby junior college also on a part-time basis. After three years, I obtained an AA degree in general education and started my first semester at San Jose State College. Before the end of the semester, Sylvia was in a family way so I quit school and took a full time job with AB Dick Co. servicing printing equipment as we started getting ready for the joyous event.

There is a seemingly innocent game which is sometimes played at wedding or baby showers. Using a simple pendulum and watching the way it moves for the one being tested you are supposed to be able to tell how many children they will have, whether they will be girls or boys, and what sequence the boys and girls will be born in. I was at the home of some friends with Sylvia when they were playing that game. Sylvia tried it and it showed that she would have a girl, a boy, a girl, then a boy. A teenage girl tried it and it showed several kids, but I don't remember how many or the sequence. Then they suggested I try it. The pendulum indicated girl, boy, girl, boy the same as for Sylvia then kept on going with the additional pattern duplicating the teenage girl's results. I had not felt any romantic feelings for this young lady before, but I began to think about the practice of polygamy which was once practiced by the church in Utah. When the girl was married a couple of years later I finally got this obsession about having her as a polygamous wife out of my system. I kept this hidden for many years, but it was a source of spiritual discomfort for me. My distaste for that obsession opened my eyes to passages in the Book of Mormon such as can be found in Jacob 1:15, "And now it came to pass that the people of Nephi, under the reign of the second king, began to grow hard in their hearts, and indulge themselves somewhat in wicked practices, such as like unto David of old desiring many wives and concubines, and also Solomon, his son."

By the way, that simple game with the pendulum would have been considered witchcraft in Old Testament times. When you start asking a pendulum for advice, rather than God you are playing with fire, for the Lord is a jealous God. On pages 369-370 of Vol. 1 of the Joseph Smith History in a letter signed by the first presidency of the church the saints were told that if "we by our wickedness, bring evil upon our own heads, the Lord will let us bear it 'til we get weary and hate iniquity." It became clear to me that the effect which thinking about polygamy with respect to that young lady had on my mind was something I needed to avoid, even to hate. For their failures, the Saints were to be scourged from city to city. The Lord tempted them with the practice of polygamy just as He tempted them with the practice of withholding the priesthood from blacks of African ancestry. We cannot come clean until we learn to hate the desire for many wives and the evils of racism. The desire for many wives hinders our ability to be guided by the Lord as does a heart full of racial hatred.

The best thing of all about our stay in the Concord area was the birth of our first daughter before we left the area. She was a beautiful baby, well fleshed out with curly blond hair. Once she could crawl, she didn't have to become very fussy during Sacrament Meeting for me to pick her up and take her out into the foyer or a hallway and play with her.

While we lived in Concord I enjoyed my job with A.B. Dick Company servicing printing equipment. The job frequently took me to the U.C. Berkeley campus where the Anti-war mobs were active and I occasionally spoke with members of the mob about their issues when things were quiet. One day I was servicing a mimeograph on the second floor of the Chancellor's office when the mob was breaking windows on the first floor. I also barely missed being at the scene when members of the mob turned over a police car and set it afire while others tossed construction steel at the police from roof tops. About this time I took a week off to help a friend who was moving to Orland, California. I spent the week helping him get his newly purchased farm ready for his family and several hundred hogs which he had been keeping on some leased land near Concord. The contrast between that peaceful country setting and U.C. Berkeley was calling me to move to an area which reminded me of my roots in Minnesota. That's when I decided to call the A.B. Dick dealer in nearby Chico to see if he had a job for me, and he did.

So, within a year or so after our first daughter was born we moved to Chico, California for a year where I worked for AB Dick Products Co. servicing duplicating equipment such as spirit duplicators, mimeographs, and offset printing presses. We attended church at Chico 2nd Ward, Gridley stake. A beautiful thing happened on the Fast Sunday after President David O. McKay passed on. I stood up and bore testimony that President Joseph Fielding Smith was rightfully our Prophet, Seer, and Revelator. I told the congregation that Joseph Fielding Smith had taught things which some members took exception to, and that I was one such member, but I knew that he was the one the Lord wanted to lead us at that time. As I bore this testimony I felt a spark of some sort of sustaining influence inside me. As I returned to my seat I felt like I was nearly floating on air. I was released from the negative spirit which had been restraining me.

In Chico 2nd Ward I was given the opportunity of being the scout leader. Though they were sometimes as wild as those march hares you hear about (I have seen jackrabbits standing on their hind legs scratching at each other with their forelegs), I enjoyed camping in the summer and playing in the snow in winter with those energetic kids. I had never been a scout, but had wandered around in the woods up to half way through my fifth year in Minnesota where I had eighty acres to use without crossing a neighbors fence. I had gone camping with my parents and with the Baptists.

My dad had shared his experiences in the backwoods of Minnesota with me. His experiences with skunks helped me keep a cool head on the one camping trip which I took the scouts on. As we were sitting on the bank of the Sacramento River after dark one slightly moon-lit evening, one of the boys called out, "Brother Porter, Brother Porter, it's a skunk!!" Deciding immediately that there was probably more danger in falling into those dark swirling waters than from the skunk I asked him in the calmest voice I could muster, "What is the skunk doing?" When the young scout replied nervously that it was rubbing against his pant leg I was relieved and assured him that if he ignored the skunk it would eventually go away. Sure enough it did.

We also took a few fishing trips with my dad along to help me with the scouts. We caught some nice bass in the backwaters behind the Oroville Dam that spring. I still talk on the phone several times a year with one of those boys even though I was their leader for barely a year.

After a year in Chico, we moved a few miles to Orland so we could attend the branch there with the Fred Olson family. Fred was serving as Branch President in the large branch which would in a few years become a Ward. Orland was a small town surrounded by farms and orchards. The Cliff Watts family had about two hundred acres of farmland and I spent a lot of time there fishing on his pond and helping him haul hay.

It wasn't long before I was the leader of the Venture Scouts, as I believe they called the older boys back then. They were old enough to want to do some shooting. I had a shotgun and cheap shells because I reloaded them myself. I also had a hand thrower for clay pigeons so we practiced together for the pheasant season coming later that year. The Watt's farm had plenty of pheasants so me and the three oldest Whitaker boys, K.C., Ron, and Bob took home a couple of birds each on opening day. The youngest son, Matthew, was not yet old enough to come along.

The Reed Whitakers became our favorite family. Besides the four boys they also had three girls, Pamela, Ann, and Patty. Their mother, Wilda Rae, minimized the use of sugar in their diets. The result was a calm, but energetic family with healthy well behaved kids. We so admired them that we asked them to be the god-parents of our children. Long after leaving Orland, we frequently made the two hour drive from Elk Grove to see them.

One evening, when I went fishing in an irrigation pond on the Percy Tracy farm I caught a 4 ½ pound largemouth bass. It provided an instant increase in my credibility with the scouts, but I'm not certain what Brother Tracy thought of the extra traffic it caused to his pond.

Even a large branch is not a place where you can expect to get by with only one calling. Soon I also became the Branch President's Executive Secretary and the financial clerk. Fortunately Sylvia was able to do most of the clerking for me so that I would have time to be the Venture Scout Leader and Executive Secretary.

I had a great deal of admiration for Fred, so when he called me to serve as his executive secretary, I opened up to our stake president, President Papas, and cleared away regrets over my past. When Fred delegated to me the responsibility of announcing a new program from SLC to the priesthood, I described it with ease. Fred said, "I never knew you could talk like that, Vern. I had a fresh start and it felt good. Better yet, our first son, Aaron, was born there.

A.B. Dick Products Co. of Chico was not owned by A.B. Dick Company so it had no big company benefits and the raises were not big enough or frequent enough. I had expected raises to come more frequently, but I was hired on the basis that I worked faster than the owners service manager. I told the owner that his man did a more thorough job than I was used to doing. He was unwilling to try to get his customers used to a lower standard of work and I agreed with him. After two years I took a job with a subsidiary of Cal Gas named Pacific Gas Equipment Company running their captive print shop on the southern edge of Sacramento, California. I got the job because they had an A.B. Dick printing press. They trusted me to upgrade their print shop with a small horizontal dark room camera, a Davidson700 offset printing press and a Chief 17 with a two color head which I used to print their catalogue, office forms and stationary, much of it for resale to propane retail outlets.

When we left Orland so I could go to work for Pacific Gas Equipment Co. we rented temporarily in Woodbridge, California near Lodi. I was soon called to be a stake missionary, then I was ordained a 70 by Franklin D. Richards back when every stake had a quorum of 70. Elder Richards gave me a powerful blessing along with the ordination.

We had a good group of 70s and stake missionaries in Lodi Ward which made my church life very pleasant. The 70's group leader was a good man. He home- taught an elderly couple whose son-in-law joined a group of polygamists and was trying to get custody of their grandchild. He told me that eight polygamists had been excommunicated in a ward not too far away. He said that all eight were either members of a ward council or were stake board members. I had thought that the polygamists were mostly in Short Creek, Arizona just over the border from Utah. Here in California they let the state welfare system take care of extra wives if the husband isn't rich enough to support them. In either case they kept their extra wives a secret so that they could be active members of the Church. The polygamists were becoming less of an irrelevant, distant phenomena.

As much as I liked Lodi Ward, the commute was proving to be time consuming, expensive, and wear and tear on the car was adding up quickly so we bought a small three bedroom home in Elk Grove, California just 10 minutes on back roads from work. Before buying the home we visited the ward it was in and found the saints very friendly and anxious to have us move in. My 70s group leader borrowed his boss's ton and ½ stake bed truck, my home teaching companion came with his station wagon, and several members of Elk Grove Ward brought their station wagons and pickups which allowed us to move with little expense. Every move we made since getting married was with the help of ward members if only to help us pack our goods and load them on a rented U-haul.

In a year or so after moving to Elk Grove our second daughter, Sarah, was born. It would take another five or six years to have our second son, Tim. Sylvia had suffered greatly with sciatica during most of her pregnancy with Sarah and she no longer ovulated so having another child didn't seem likely. The sciatic pains persisted after Sarah's birth. Chiropractic adjustments gave some relief for awhile, then seemed to make the pain worse so we tried an Osteopathic Physician who treated her with something he called auricular therapy. The physician was referred to us by Sylvia's stepfather and his practice was seventy five miles away. We made the trip regularly until my work hours changed. At this point I received some training in foot reflexology. The reflexology treatments gave Sylvia some relief so I continued administering them to Sylvia for several years. During this time Sylvia still was not ovulating so when I worked on the areas of her feet which were marked off on the foot reflexology charts as being for sciatica I also worked on the areas shown to be for her ovaries. I did this several times per week for over five years as her sciatic pains gradually diminished.

Nearly six years after Sarah's birth, Sylvia thought she might be pregnant. She went to her doctor to see what he could tell her. He was surprised to discover she was pregnant without having had any indications of ovulating for so many years. Tim was carried to term with little or no sciatic problems for Sylvia.

Financially, life was challenging in Elk Grove as it had been in Orland and Chico, but in every other way life was good. I made use of my training with AB Dick by servicing printing equipment evenings and Saturdays in order to get a little slack in our budget. I did join a gun club in order to use their pistol range, but didn't feel I could afford to use their trap shooting range and I hadn't found a place where I could use my clay pigeon thrower.

We found a local dairy that sold raw milk a little cheaper than the pasteurized milk at the local stores. If things were tight we mixed it with powdered milk. We skimmed off the cream and saved it until we had enough to make homemade ice cream. I had planted lots of strawberries which we ate with the ice cream, on pancakes and waffles or with only a little milk and sugar. We bought fruit from local orchards for canning and eating fresh. In order to stretch the budget when I was working for AmeriGas/Cal Gas, Sylvia sewed some of our clothes. She was a great homemaker and with the finances also since she had a Bachelor's Degree in business from San Francisco State University. In church, she served as the Ward Librarian, the Ward Organist and sometimes sang solos. Being blessed with personality plus, she was a trophy wife.

In the mean time, my progressive nerve disease had resulted in severe hammer toes which caused corns on the toes and the balls of my feet. Walking was very painful, but I put off surgery for several years until we had good enough health insurance to cover most of the expenses.

We had a bishop who pushed hard to obtain some extra donations beyond fast offering and tithing from ward members. He called us in and announced that he and his councilors had been praying to know how much to ask of us and thereupon told us what was expected. We explained that in spite of the economy measures we used it was difficult to meet all of our needs at the present level of donations. He wanted us to increase our donations anyway and suggested that he could give us funds from the Church or send us to Deseret Industries in order to obtain shoes occasionally. In other words, he was willing to make us objects of charity if we would increase our donations so that he would not have to admit that he was not inspired when he decided what our donations should be. We were already paying tithing, fast offering and donating for other purposes.

We were fully involved in the Latter-Day Saint life and enjoying our LDS friends and church activities. However, of a growing concern was the racist attitudes and Brigham Young's doctrine. A friend living in another stake had a set of the *Journal of Discourses* and he showed me some of the radical doctrine Brigham had taught. I started saving so I could buy a set of my own, but was too busy to be distracted by Brigham Young's doctrine at the time. It wasn't long before I was one of the Sacramento South Stake's seven presidents of the 70.

Somehow I managed to find time for church league basketball most years. I didn't like the "win at all costs" attitudes of many of the players. We hired professional referees, and they did not like it either. Our league had a bad reputation with the refs, far too much fouling on purpose in order to throw a player off his game and too much in the way of bad tempers.

I had some close friendships developing in the Sacramento area. One of them made no attempt to hide his fascination with polygamy even though he already had a lovely wife and some beautiful children. There was a young lady in the area for whom he was fond. When he told me she was marrying a relative of his I saw a little sadness in his eyes. Then he added, "at least she'll be in the family". That worried me. The fact that someone was teaching the single adults that the sisters would not be held as accountable for sex sin as would the men added to my concerns about polygamy. Another favorite saying in some circles was, "if you are righteous enough you may be asked to do something which was previously considered evil." They liked to point to Abraham's willingness to offer up Isaac, but they failed to mention that in the end God provided a ram in Isaac's place and that slaying an innocent child for a sacrifice was and is still considered evil.

Cal Gas was in the propane business, and the propane business was in the step-sister sector of the petroleum industry so here again the prospect of raising a family on Cal-Gas pay didn't seem encouraging and I moved on to 3M Company servicing printing equipment after a few years. When I left Pacific Gas Equipment Company for 3M the out of town travel made it difficult to keep up with my Seventy's Presidency duties so I asked to be released and became the teacher of the Investigator Class.

In the mean time I was enjoying teaching the Investigator Class, but concerned about the effort to make the church a haven for racists. This was about 1975 and the priesthood did not become available to men of all races until 1978. Racists were sometimes told by certain members, "you ought to join the LDS Church, we know how to keep the Blacks in their place." I told the class, "It appears to me that we are much too proud of the fact that the Blacks are not allowed to hold the priesthood. The black skin is not the curse of Cain and they aren't poison to the Temple, they can be baptized for the dead in them." I didn't have the slightest idea that I was in trouble. The following weekend my mom and dad were visiting. They had brought along their Sunday clothes and came to church with us to attend the Investigator Class and hear me teach. As we entered the classroom we saw to our surprise that someone else was already at the chalkboard getting ready to teach the lesson. Afterwards my group leader told me that one of the investigators hated blacks and had complained to a friend who had some influence in the Church. That influence was strong enough to have someone else take over as teacher of the class. I certainly didn't want to get caught in a conflict involving people of unknown influence in the Church so I let it go for awhile. In the meantime I started studying into the midnight hours every night and taking notes from the scriptures, the Church histories and the *Journal of Discourses*. I did this for several years.

As I was developing a skeptical attitude I became the chief agitator in the Seventy's group meetings in our ward. At one of those meetings my leader told me in front of the group, "You had better shape up or I'm going to run you out of the church." I eventually complained to the Stake President, with no results. A few years later I asked the Stake President why he hadn't done anything about my complaints. His reply was simply, "I knew you were sensitive to your leaders so I discounted much of what you said". What a pitiful excuse for considering me a liar. A better excuse was the fact that my group leader was rumored to have business dealings with one of the stake president's counselors.

The stench of racism and polygamy troubled my mind. As I started studying into the late hours of the night and taking notes I soon found that our commentaries by Church scholars and past and living general authorities of the church were mistaken in their denials of false teachings by Brigham Young, more about that later. The High Council advisor to the 70 was a good man so I went to him for advice. He sent me to an Instructor in the Church Institute of Religion for advice. I threw everything at him I had found in the *Journal of Discourses, the History of the Church*, a six volume set and a seven volume set, and the scriptures. He seemed to be familiar with all of it, but all he would say was, "I know the Church is true". It had become obvious that there was something wrong in the Church and it was being hidden from the general membership with the help of our scholars and some of our leaders.

Also hidden from the general membership of the Church was several decades of progress in the Church's efforts to accommodate blacks. I just recently read a biography on David O. McKay which wasn't published until 2005. I must say that it was very encouraging to find that he considered the withholding of the priesthood merely a practice, not a doctrine. He saw to it that the Fijian's ancestry was examined so that they could receive the priesthood when no connection to Africa was discovered in their genealogy. He did away with the practice of withholding the priesthood from South African whites who could not show where their ancestors came from some other continent. He also put a stop to the practice of preventing temple marriages to couples wherein black ancestry was rumored, but not proven. As much as he wanted to see the blacks get the priesthood, his many attempts to obtain revelation on that subject failed. One of his counselors told him that the saints were not ready for that to happen. Yet when it did happen, the rumors had it that it was only because of political pressure that the announcement was made or, on the other hand, that the popular miniseries ROOTS was a sign that blacks were ready for the priesthood.

Because the above efforts by David O. McKay were not generally known some of my brethren hadn't forgiven me for confronting racists. Perhaps some of them think members like me are partially responsible for the change in policy. Some of them would like to run me out of the Church so that they could add Sylvia to their harems in the hereafter. This was true twenty five years ago and is still true now that I have come back to the Church.

Just flat out leaving the Church was out of the question as I had a testimony of the Gospel proclaimed by Joseph Smith. Performing my Home Teaching responsibilities was something I had enjoyed, but my mixed feelings about Brigham Young's teachings took a lot of joy out of it. Living with the lies was tearing me apart. Knowing something had to be done I decided to check out the Reorganized Church of Jesus Christ of Latter-Day Saints since they were the only other sizeable group to survive the assassination of Joseph Smith. The Reorganized Church has two congregations in the Sacramento area. I became acquainted with Jack Wight who had a local leadership position in the Reorganized Church. He was a descendant of a prominent member of the Church back before Joseph Smith was assassinated and he was very knowledgeable about Church history. I was very impressed by him and the members of the RLDS Church he soon had me associating with.

At this time, I thought I understood the New Testament passage saying that the wheat and tares should grow up together until it was time to gather the tares for burning. Coming face to face with the power of the tares in the Church was a source of great concern. Going into our history and discovering how much power they had from the beginning of the restoration was something for which I was not ready. During years of missionary work I had been telling non-members that the Church was perfect. I could no longer be a party to the cover-ups and lies. The Church contains a wide variety of peoples and my experiences with them are also varied. When it comes to turning the stakes of Zion into a pure people, Brigham Young had something to say about that. Nov 9, 1856, JD vol. 4, p77; "There are many of the men and women now before me who have looked for a pure people, and have supposed that that was a proof of the truth of our doctrines, but they will never find such a people until Satan is bound, and Jesus comes to reign with his Saints. ... I have many a time, in this stand, dared the world to produce as mean devils as we can; we can beat them at anything. We have the greatest and smoothest liars in the world, the cunningest and most adroit thieves, and any other shade of character that you can mention." As much as I was disgusted by Brigham Young's heresies his frankness was refreshing.

[In the October conference of 2013 President Ochtdorf said something like, the Church cannot be perfect until the members are perfect. I see some hopeful signs occasionally.]

CHAPTER 10

TO HELL AND BACK

I was welcomed into the RLDS Church by some great people. When the local stake president of the LDS Church became aware of my joining the RLDS Church he called me before the Stake High Council to be excommunicated. I became a very active member of the RLDS Church for a couple of years, but it soon became evident that those great people in that Church who had impressed me were not in tune with the leadership of the Reorganized Church and soon they were meeting in private homes instead of attending the regular meetings in RLDS Chapels. The leadership of the RLDS Church was leading its followers on a path aimed at making good press and good relations with the Ecumenical movement more important than sticking up for the Book of Mormon and the Prophet Joseph Smith's proclamation of the restoration of priesthood authority.

While I was active in the RLDS Church, I jointly taught a Sunday School class with a member of one of the priesthood quorums. After writing a letter to the editor of the Saint's Herald, I exchanged some letters with members of the First Presidency including Wallace B. Smith and Allan D. Tyree. My letters were very critical of some articles in the Saint's Herald and the Temple School materials. The presidency was very supportive of what they referred to as "diversity". I told one of their visiting authorities that it looked to me like they were attempting to make the Church a safe place for atheists and agnostics, but a very uncomfortable place for those of us who take the scriptures seriously.

I quit attending on a regular basis and started taking Sylvia to her Sacrament Meetings and Church socials. Just to be with her more often I also sometimes sang in the choir of whatever ward we lived in. Now I was alienated from both churches and angry at God to boot. Being away from home so much was hard on family life so I decided I needed a job with no requirement for travel. After a short stint with Cable Data I ended up back at PGEC, the subsidiary of Cal Gas. By the time my progressive nerve disease made it necessary to become a client of the California Department of Rehabilitation, I had worked for two other Cal Gas/AmeriGas entities, namely, PACA and the Cal Gas/AmeriGas terminals department.

As a client of the Department of Rehabilitation for a couple of years, I finally became a permanent/intermittent state employee working 5-6 hours per day several days per week. Only two hours at most were pain free. When I got home from work I worked on writing my first book. The last couple of years I also wrote for the Elk Grove Citizen covering a wide variety of stories including an occasional item of hard news.

Suffice it to say that my life was busy, filled with physical pain and anger which I hid behind a lot of joking around. My humor was often self-effacing, but sometimes a little cutting when aimed at others which was on rare occasion a little hurtful for those who didn't know me well enough.

Being married to an apostate was beginning to wear on Sylvia to the point that I began to recognize the signs. If we were not in agreement and I said, "I can whip you.", I began to notice an edge in her voice when she replied, "You better not.", so I changed my tactics and said instead, "I can spank you and I like to spank you baby". That made a difference. It pained me to see Sylvia's attitude towards me and life in general cause her pain. It became obvious that our relationship needed help so I planned a party for our 40th wedding anniversary. We invited family and a few friends to Mimi's for a dinner.

Sylvia worked in a dental office, first for Dr. Bell, then when he retired, for Dr. Jeffery Chantry. Whenever I stopped by the office I would say something like, "All right, where is she? I want to know where that good looking woman is every minute of the day." I was soon hearing Sylvia's friends tell her what a great guy she had. I would often laugh it off with, "It's nothing I can brag about, I was born that way." While I was a good boy as a child, I know what kind of man I might have grown up to become had not the Lord intervened and taken my athleticism away from me. As much as I wanted to be athletic, I was grateful for that beating I took, if that is what caused the decline in my athleticism, and I often thank the Lord for saving my soul from Hell.

As a little gratitude came into my heart I began to have some vivid dreams. This was after I had retired early at the age of 62. In my dreams I was either working for A.B. Dick or 3M Co. again, and it varied from night to night. In my dreams I was in a panic because I was behind in fulfilling my service contract work and I thought I was going to be fired. I would wake up in a panic thinking I needed to look for work, even though I was already retired. Then occasionally I would dream I was in the mission field and in trouble with the Lord because I hadn't been doing my missionary work. I was doing a very good job of ignoring those dreams until my four year old grand-daughter, Alana, started singing "I am a child of God" as she was sitting on my lap. A couple of times I joined in singing with her and my heart was melted and I became concerned about the kind of example I was setting for my children and grandchildren. I began to wonder how I could ever have thought that the Lord would give up on the Latter-Day Saints after only a few decades when He had stuck by the Children of Israel for hundreds of years. As I began to wonder about rejoining the church an evil presence entered my dreams trying to make me feel unworthy. When I decided I would come back, he left my dreams. I have rarely had such vivid dreams as I did back then.

The fact that someone wanted me to come back to the church and the Devil wanted me to feel unworthy to come back reinforced my desire to do it. I had promised myself that I would not come back until there were some serious changes in the Church. I had to face the fact that I had been a fool in thinking the Lord would abandon the Saints after only a few decades. Though there had been some changes in the church, I would soon find out just how little some members had changed.

Some how the word spread that I was being rebaptized and when the day came, there was standing room only, even with heavy curtains opened to make the room larger. It was very reassuring and I was grateful to see so many old friends in attendance. One of my scouts from Chico Ward, Bart Williams, came all the way from Texas to be there. Reed Whitaker, from Orland, and his son K.C. were there. Of course Rich Barney, his wife Holly, his mother Doreen, his sister Janet and her husband Mark Sylvester came up from the Bay Area.

Sylvia gave a talk at Sacrament Meeting one Sunday shortly after I came back to the church. With mixed emotions I listened to a talk as good as one hears during general conference. I was at the same time grateful that my excommunication had not dragged her down and made her ashamed because of my failings. My heart swelled with gratitude for the great lady who has stuck by me and I wondered what I could do to deserve her. It gives me great pleasure to see the improvement in her outlook on life since I started trying to win back her affection and confidence in me. In the evening when we relax in front of the television I glance over and notice that whether she is doing a little sewing or recreational reading, she has a pleasant smile on her face. How grateful I am to the Lord for bringing me back to the Church.

I was grateful, but there were some members who had not forgiven me for making my stand against racism in the Church and/or the modern practice of polygamy in California. I must acknowledge that nearly all of the great many acquaintances I have in the church have been very supportive of me and glad to see me come back. However, the first time I made a comment in High Priest's group meeting with which they were not familiar some of those around me started murmuring their disagreement. A few weeks later a member of the High Council said the same thing and received nothing but "amens". It was evidence for me that some Latter-Day Saints were respecters of persons and didn't know the truth when they heard it.

My first Bishop after I returned to the Church was concerned about seeing that I fit in with the ward members so he called me to serve as the Ward Historian which meant I was able to associate with members of the Ward Council on a regular basis in order to collect histories of the auxiliary and priesthood organizations. This was very helpful in getting me back into the spirit of things. I was a witness to plans for the various auxiliary and priesthood organizations and reports on their successes. Very often there were assignments to help someone move in or out or within the ward. Sometimes it was an opportunity to volunteer to help a widow or elderly man with a project around his/her home, perhaps even repairing a leaky roof or fixing a problem with plumbing. Recently a member of the ward council mentioned that a neighbor of his told him that the denomination he belonged to needed some help widening the driveway for their meeting house parking lot. The Elder's Quorum President offered to help this local protestant Church and the Bishop agreed that it would be a good thing if volunteers were sought to help with the project.

It was comforting to discover that a member of the stake high council who lived in my ward also had my back. Those steel folding chairs we had to sit on during priesthood meeting were very uncomfortable so Sylvia sewed me a cushion for the seat and one for the back of those chairs. He must have sensed the ribbing which might come my way over using those cushions because the moment he noticed me using them he said, "Vern is the smartest one in the room." If some of the other nonsense I had to put up with is an indication, he saved from a lot of ribbing. He likely sensed that my past problems in the Church might make me a little sensitive to what might only be normal kidding around.

It didn't take long to figure out that there was a target on my back. All it took was requesting some consideration for us older priesthood holders. The metal folding chairs we sat on during our priesthood meetings caused a great deal of discomfort to some of us older brethren with flabby posteriors and I could tell that I wasn't the only one. Because of my long legs all of my weight was distributed over a much smaller portion of my anatomy than for shorter folks, making it even more difficult for me to endure the pain near my tail bone.

Our ward was the last ward in the building that season (three wards shared the building) which meant that the chapel was empty during our priesthood meeting. All the quorums gathered together for opening exercises before separating for quorum activities. The older Elders, of which I was one, met with the High Priests so I suggested that the High Priest group meet in the chapel where we could set on padded pews or even in the very comfortable choir seats. The Bishop was taking care of business in his office so his counselors were in charge. They said they would talk it over with the Elders quorum president and the High Priest group leader. The following week when they announced it was time to go to our class rooms they said that the Elders would be meeting in the chapel and the High Priests would go to their usual classroom with steel folding chairs. I stood up and indignantly demanded to know who had decided that and why. They had made it obvious what they thought of me, but they reconsidered by the next Sunday and finally us older priesthood brethren got to set through our meetings in relative comfort, but it was clear that I had ruffled some feathers. As the schedules change every year, we are the last ward in the building only one year in three, but how we look forward to that year.

Saying the wrong thing was not quite a habit, but was occasionally difficult to avoid. It had been over twenty years since I had studied the scriptures, but I didn't immediately go back to the notes I had taken before I left the Church, instead I started over by studying the scriptures in connection with Sunday School Class and Priesthood Class. Because Sacramento is a college town Sylvia and I attended adult Institute of Religion classes provided by the Church every semester. At an adult Institute class on the scriptures when the atonement came up, it was stated that when Jesus bled from every pore in the Garden He was atoning for our sins. I had always believed that the Savior paid for my sins by taking my place on the cross so I sarcastically reported my relief at discovering that He didn't die on the cross for me. He only had to shed a drop of blood in the Garden on my behalf.

During a conversation outside of class with a very strict member of the Church I said, "I think it's kind of silly to imagine that it took four tries for the Lord to atone for our sins, three times in the Garden and once on the Cross". He immediately worked himself into an indignant state of mind as he told me I was denying the very basis of the Church. I thought I was about to be called before the High Council. That made me more than a little uneasy about someone I considered a friend.

Recently, the second counselor to President Monson, Dieter F. Uchtdorf, said at the Priesthood session of the October, 2013 Conference, regarding those who leave the Church "Sometimes we assume it is because they have been offended or are lazy or sinful. Actually, it is not that simple. In fact, there is not just one reason that applies to the variety of situations." One of the categories he spoke of was the mistakes of imperfect people. "And, to be perfectly frank, there have been times when members or leaders in the Church have simply made mistakes."

While the great majority of local Latter-Day Saints have been really great, some few have displayed attitudes like the example President Uchtdorf told us was too simple. I have been accused in priesthood meeting of leaving the Church because my feelings had been hurt and I could not forgive. Another time someone who is known to have known me for a long time said, "It has been my experience that when someone leaves the Church it is because they are guilty of serious sin, but I don't mean Vern, of course." That's the kind of thing sneaky lawyers say to the jury knowing it will be stricken, but will have its influence. Some of our local leaders and members think they know so much more than do our general authorities.

After being active in the Church for a year after my rebaptism, I was eligible to have my blessings restored which means that if they considered my repentance sufficient my standing in the Church would once more be just like it had been before I apostatized over 25 years ago. I was required to write a letter to President Monson expressing my desire to have my blessing restored and explaining why I thought I deserved it. When I wrote my letter I chose not to withhold anything which might later be held against me so I explained that my testimony does not require me to believe that all of our leaders have been true to their callings and that I did not consider the Pearl of Great Price completely credible. When President Monson sent a member of the Quorum of Seventy to restore my blessings I repeated those things about my testimony to him. He did not rebuke me or tell me that my testimony marked me as unworthy.

While attending an adult Institute of Religion class shortly after having my blessings restored, I mentioned the above experience because I felt the example of tolerance given by President Monson and the Seventy who restored my blessings was worthy of note. But, someone in the class knew better and I endured an exchange of emails from a brother who felt it his duty to make me feel that my testimony was sorely lacking because he felt that it had to be all or nothing when it comes to believing the standard works of the Church. Some local leaders and members desire to hold me to a higher standard than do the general authorities.

A year or so later, I stood up in Fast and Testimony Meeting and told the congregation how I had stood up against racism and the then current secret practice of polygamy in California. I told them how the bad treatment I received caused me to get involved in an intense study of our history which resulted in my discovery of things which led me to believe that the Lord had cast off the Latter-Day Saints. Consequently, I left the Church for twenty five years. After the meeting I noticed that some of the Saints were more friendly towards me and some were less so. The "All is well in Zion" crowd got rougher with me than the racists did over 25 years ago.

I was scheduled to give a talk in Sacrament Meeting soon. Before the time came, I discovered that reactions to my testimony had reached people with influence in the Stake. Someone told me I should show the Bishop and the Stake President copies of my talk for approval because of the passion I displayed in that testimony, or so they said. It was obvious that they had no intention of telling me who was stabbing me in the back and they did not have the courage of their convictions or they would have told me just what it was in my testimony that they didn't like. If being passionate in giving one's testimony was good reason to make one feel scrutinized a lot of members would not be able to give a talk without it being approved. They obviously wanted to destroy my self confidence and they didn't mind lying to me.

I'm not surprised that I wasn't allowed to give the talk. It contained more truth than some of the Saints are ready for, although I did not include the things which I had found to be very upsetting. I eventually discovered the reason at least one member didn't like my testimony. He said it was inappropriate because in was about things in the past. He is apparently of that same mind set as those who prefer to cover up our past.

The opposition I faced was hard on my self-confidence, but the Lord helped me with that when I was asked to administer a blessing to someone who had been in an accident. I'm afraid I am lacking in faith to be healed. I sometimes entertain feelings that I deserve the bad health which robs me of strength because of the many years I was angry at the Lord. When I first came back to the Church I was shuffling around like an old man. I don't have good balance so I still have to be careful. Though I am stronger than I was when I came back to the Church about six years ago, the damage which has been done to my wrists and my lack of stamina still seriously restricts my activities. Whether or not I accept a home teaching assignment depends not only upon my stamina, but also upon how the saints who read this book respond to me after reading it. I don't dare entertain high hopes after what some of them have already put me through, but that is alright. I came back so that I could be a good example to my children and my grandchildren. That my beloved wife is much happier now has made it all worthwhile. One of my favorite sayings about these so-called golden years is that being a broken down old fart is worthwhile because of my kids, and grandchildren and the fact that my wife still loves me and sticks by me.

It has been about six years since I was rebaptized and it has been busy. I am back and ready to fight for my beliefs. Doing so without doing harm to the testimonies of the other members requires caution so I often bite my tongue during Sunday School Class. I recently threw caution to the wind in Sunday School class and talked about the false doctrine which figured in my leaving the Church. I didn't tell the class that Brigham Young was the source of that false doctrine. The last one to speak to that class remarked "That goes to show that you shouldn't listen to things people claim to be doctrine." Later, when I passed him in the hall, he gave me a very friendly self-satisfied smile. I'll bet more Baptists than Mormons know about Brigham Young's false doctrine.

On a Saturday evening while watching television after a busy day, we experienced an electrical surge. In the air conditioner closet we heard some snapping and popping as smoke began pouring out of our VCR and lights began fading on and off. After turning off all the power strips I turned off the main breaker, opened the doors, and called the fire department. After going through the house and attic one of the firemen told us we would have to leave the house until an electrician could make it safe. As our plight became known we received invitations to stay in the homes of ward members. Sylvia was praying for an electrician when a friend dropped by and assured the fireman in charge that he would make certain it was safe for us to remain in the house before he left. It was nearly midnight before he left. On Sunday, after teaching a class at church, he was a member of our ward, he showed up about noon to continue checking for burned wiring. He also called S.M.U.D. (our local power provider) out and they made temporary repairs to the incoming electrical service line where it had been damaged by tree branches and/or rodents and by late evening we had power to the house once more.

It's good to be around so many Latter-Day Saints who are really great people. They are a happy, hard working people and few of them show any results of the persecution in the history of the Church. Unfortunately, one of the symptoms is looking at those who disagree with them as enemies. The result for those few in that category is the shutdown of their nurturing mode. When you disagree with one of their favorite beliefs they will turn into critics instead of trying to change your mind. Yes, Latter-Day Saints are a cross section of everyday people and some of them behave like radical political activists who come face to face with solid opposition.

CHAPTER 11

THE EFFORT TO TURN THE CHURCH INTO A CULT

There is a game of one-ups-man-ship being played in the Church by the overly ambitious who are power hungry. An old example involves the Word of Wisdom. Every few years there used to be someone who wanted to expand the list of things to avoid or lose your temple recommend. Back when racism ruled the day, someone occasionally came out with a better explanation so they thought for withholding the priesthood from blacks of African descent. About a century ago, some of our leaders decided to show us how they could improve the Biblical account of the Savior's last time in the Garden of Gethsemane. Disagreeing with the expanded view of what occurred in the Garden can bring accusations of heresy it did in my case after I returned to the Church.

A misunderstanding of the scriptures has allowed some members and leaders to imagine that when they have an idea without their minds being darkened, they can consider the idea revelation. The result sometimes is solid doctrine being replaced by fables. I'm suggesting that when our youth start thinking for themselves some of them learn to see through these fables and their testimonies are damaged.

The scripture in question is in D&C 9 and concerns Oliver Cowdery's failure to translate the gold plates when given the opportunity. Oliver was told that his bosom would burn within him if he translated properly, but his mind would be darkened if it was wrong. This is a gift which will elude those who don't have a true and solid understanding of the gospel. It will elude those who look beyond the mark and seek things which are hard to understand and they will come to despise the words of plainness. This is why so many believed that blacks of African descent could not be given the priesthood for so many years and would not during their mortal lives. This is why so many don't understand that the Book of Mormon is against polygamy and that the revelation on polygamy (D&C 132) contradicts the Book of Mormon and the Law of Moses. This is why so many don't understand what we lost when we were driven out of Missouri.

It is important to understand that what we lost when we were scourged from city to city until we arrived in Utah was the result of failing a test. The Lord said He would test us to see if we believed the Book of Mormon. Being scourged from city to city was punishment for failing the test. We lost our commission to establish the Zion of God in Jackson County Missouri. In 1855 Brigham Young told the Saints they still had the same authority in conferences that they always had. Until the Saints were deprived of meeting in general conference by Joseph Smith in Nauvoo, as far as I can tell the rights they enjoyed were as described by Brigham Young in Great Salt Lake City, October 6, 1855, JD, Vol. 3, p.44; "They [the Saints] are to judge not only men, they are to be judges not only in the capacity of a Conference to decide what shall be done, what course shall be pursued to further the kingdom of God, what business shall be transacted, and how it shall be transacted, and so on…"

Later on in that same talk (p. 45), Brigham Young emphasized the importance of the Saints knowing for themselves that the kingdom was properly organized; "Suppose that the people were heedless, that they manifested no concern with regard to the things of the kingdom of God, but threw the whole burden upon the leaders of the people, saying,

'If the brethren who take charge of matters are satisfied, we are,' this is not pleasing in the sight of the Lord."

"Every man and woman in this kingdom ought to be satisfied with what we do, but they never should be satisfied without asking the Father, in the name of Jesus Christ, whether what we do is right. When you are inspired by the Holy Ghost you can understandingly say, that you are satisfied; and that is the only power that should cause you to exclaim that you are satisfied, for without that you do not know whether you should be satisfied or not."

However, Brigham delivered mixed messages regarding the voice of the conference. September 30, 1860 (JD Vol. 8, p. 189), speaking of Joseph Smith, Brigham Young said; "The people required him to be as holy as the Almighty himself, and to never make a mistake. Wherein the First Presidency and the Twelve do wrong, it is not in the ability of the people to detect them in those wrongs. ... if they commit an error, it is passed over, and the people cannot tell wherein or when, or how to correct it."

The Church is so much bigger now. I see no reason to complain about the fact that the general authorities take care of the worldwide business of the Church without input from the rest of the Church. With the modern means of communication available to us now it could be done, but we are living during the days when the wheat and tares should grow together. This is not yet a time for establishing the Zion of God or thinking we should be attempting to be caught up to the City of Enoch as a group.

The general authorities establish guidelines for the local business of the Church. At the local level the various leadership meetings give ample opportunity for quorum and auxiliary groups to work out the details of their planning within the guidelines from the general authorities. As a Ward Historian I attended ward council meetings and I can tell you that the work of the Lord is accomplished because of the decisions made at such meetings.

So, though I acknowledge that the general membership may not yet be capable of providing guidance for the workings of the Church at large, some of us can tell when general authorities are giving us speculative doctrine which is not consistent with the scriptures. The idea, for instance, that our modern general authorities have a better understanding of atonement than did Peter, James, John, and Paul is a heady proposition. But, here we are with the doctrine of Jesus atoning for our sins in the Garden of Gethsemane becoming much too popular in my estimation. In the last couple of months I have heard several times the testimony from a Bishop and a member of the stake high council as follows, "I testify that Jesus performed the holy atonement in the Garden, then He was crucified". It has become so popular that when I made fun of the idea that it took Jesus four tries to atone for our sins, three times in the Garden and once on the cross, it became obvious that I was in trouble. I was told by someone in my stake in a threatening manner, that the idea that Jesus atoned for our sins in the Garden was the basis of our religion. But, the message of atonement in the Bible is that the Savior would be punished instead of us with no mention of the idea that He could atone for our sins by merely feeling the weight of them or feeling anguish for them.

Jesus demonstrated his ability to forgive sin just by saying so, but He agreed to pay the price of sin for those who would follow him. Mosiah, chapter 15 clearly explains whom Jesus died for. When did the doctrine of atonement in the Garden become revelation? Our general authorities cannot even agree on the details. Elder Talmage taught that Jesus atoned for all the sins of humanity from Adam to the final judgment, but Tad R. Callister is teaching that the Savior atoned for all the sins of creation infinitely into the past and future. A member of the Stake gave me a copy of Callister's *THE INFINITE ATONEMENT* expecting it would convince me of the error of my ways. In describing the Savior's suffering and bleeding in the Garden and on the cross, Tad R. Callister on page 132 of *THE INFINITE ATONEMENT* concludes, "The full price would be paid. Every sin of Sodom, Gomorrah, Babylon, your sins and mine, would be accounted for, suffered for, and paid for before the Savior would choose to let death in."

Regarding the sacrifices for atonement offered under the Law of Moses, atonement is mentioned frequently. But, why is the word "atonement" only used once in the New Testament and reconcile or reconciliation used instead? Why is "infinite atonement" used so often in the Book of Mormon? Why did the Jews look forward to a day of salvation and why did so many go to be baptized by John the Baptist?

The answer is that the ritual atonement of the Old Testament did not reconcile to God those who committed sin because the sacrifices and judgments of the Law of Moses offered no promise of eternal life. Ritual sacrifice did not replace the harsh punishments of the Law of Moses. However, the atonement Jesus offered promised eternal life in the presence of God to those who qualified while the atonement of the Old Testament merely offered good standing in God's temporary, earthly, mortal kingdom. There is, therefore, an infinite difference between the atonement offered under the Law of Moses and the atonement offered by Jesus. The Book of Mormon peoples were obsessed with the difference because they were living under the Law of Moses even after they were told about Jesus. The early apostles in the land of Jerusalem lived to see the promise of reconciliation to God so they rightfully concentrated on that. Thus, the Savior's sacrifice is the main topic of the New Testament and "reconcile" is the term used therein.

As the author of the law the death of our sinless Lord can be looked upon as providing an infinite atonement, but it cannot pay for sins which perpetrators will not give up. Call it atonement or reconciliation, it's a bargain we make in order to become joint-heirs with Jesus. We give up those things which He disapproves of and He pays the penalty demanded for our past sins by his being punished instead of us. Jesus died once for all of us and by His resurrection we are all resurrected. That is the one benefit of the Savior's death which is universal, but it is not atonement. Atonement is associated with the New Testament or Covenant. Atonement is for heirs. Forgiveness of sin is for heirs. Atonement and refusal to repent are mutually exclusive. We are born into bodies which will die because our first parents, Adam and Eve transgressed and we agreed to be born into bodies which will die. We do not need to have our sins forgiven in order to be resurrected for the unrepentant must suffer for their sins until the final judgment when they will be ressurected.

The idea that Jesus volunteered to feel anguish in the Garden for the wickedness and abominations of all people in order to atone for their sins is as silly as the old sectarian practice of self flagellation for the purpose of creating a store of merit to augment the Savior's atonement. The Book of Mormon passage about the Savior's anguish in the Garden did not stipulate that atonement was involved. The D&C reference to the Savior's suffering in the Garden was mentioned merely for the purpose of comparing His suffering in the Garden to the suffering the wicked will experience as they await the final judgment. The teaching that Jesus atoned for our sins in the Garden is speculation which goes against the Biblical teachings on that subject.

Those who claim that Jesus was atoning for all the sins of creation infinitely into the past and future may fail to recognize that such a claim creates a serious obstacle to the principle of "eternal progression". If there are to be future generations of spirit children born, they will repeat the history of Earth. If Jesus already atoned for all the sins of creation infinitely into the past and future then there will be no need for another Son of God to atone for their sins. Jesus explained the process very clearly in John 5:19-20

19) "Then answered Jesus and said unto them, Verily, verily, I say unto you, The Son can do nothing of himself, but what he seeth the Father do: for what things soever he doeth, these also doeth the Son likewise.
20) For the Father loveth the Son, and sheweth him all things that himself doeth: and he will shew him greater works than these, that ye may marvel."

For me the fact that the belief that Jesus was atoning for our sins in the Garden is not mentioned in the Bible tells me that said doctrine comes under the category of looking beyond the mark. The result is doctrine which is difficult to understand. Trying to make it look like Latter-Day general authorities are smarter than the apostles and prophets in the Bible tells me that all is not well in Zion and that is all right with me because the Book of Mormon warns us against thinking that "all is well in Zion, yea Zion prospereth." However, there is a clique which is easily offended by any hint that all is not well in Zion. I have been in their faces. They need to forgive me and get over it or they will find that they are guilty of the greater sin.

The Apostle Paul told the Corinthians in chapter 11, verse 19, "For there must be also heresies among you, that they which are approved may be made manifest among you." President Ochtdorf in October of 2013 admitted that he supposed the Church could not be perfect while there were imperfect people in it. Well, I don't mind being among imperfect people, the Lord knows I am far from perfect, but I do mind being around self-righteous snobs who look down their noses at me because I don't respect their speculations.

When the Savior was crucified, his death brought an end to the law of dead works. Because He was the author of the Law, His death fulfilled the Law and because His death fulfilled the Law, the atonement He accomplished must be viewed as an infinite atonement. An atonement which paid for the sins of the unrepentant would be more than infinite, it would be impossible, a contradiction in terms. His resurrection established his credentials for glorifying all those who reject the sins of the flesh. They are qualified to become joint-heirs with Him because their rejection of sin marks them as the only ones for whom the Lord's atonement could count. Those who refuse to repent must maintain ownership of their sins and bear the punishment for them.

Why would anyone ask the Savior to suffer for the sins of the unrepentant when they are required to suffer for their own sins. In both the New Testament and the Book of Mormon Jesus made it clear that He was not praying for the world, but only for those whom the Father had given him. Why would the Lord suffer for each and every sin of each and every member of the whole world when He would not even pray for each and every member of the whole world?

Regarding those who must suffer for their own sins, many are saying that the unrepentant must atone for their own sins, but the scripture merely says that they must suffer for them. Those who receive the benefit of atonement get to be with Jesus in the hereafter. That means that they are heirs of Celestial or Terrestrial glory. Those who must suffer for their own sins can receive no greater glory than the telestial and that only if they can and want to live the laws of that kingdom. They can be heirs of salvation, but can their suffering really be called atonement if they aren't allowed to be in the Terrestrial Kingdom where Jesus presides or the Celestial kingdom where Jesus resides? Not in the fullest sense of the word. In the telestial glory they are presided over by the Holy Ghost and cannot go to the Terrestrial Kingdom where Jesus presides or the Celestial Kingdom where Jesus dwells.

In 2nd Timothy 4:3-4 we are warned of a time when people "will not endure sound doctrine ... and shall heap to themselves teachers, having itching ears; And they shall turn away their ears from the truth and shall be turned unto fables." In Luke 11:42 the Savior warned of those who would tithe mint and rue and all manner of herb, and pass over judgment and the love of God. In verse 43 He told of those who love the uppermost seats in the synagogues. I have seen modern versions of the above recently. Jesus warned his followers in Matthew 10:16, "Behold, I send you forth as sheep in the midst of wolves: be ye therefore wise as serpents, and harmless as doves." It has been my experience that some of the brethren think that being wise as serpents means turning the word of God into fables if they think it will give them some advantage and a reason to look down their noses at those who don't share their enthusiasm for speculation. In the Church we are living among those who are the true followers of Christ and among those who by their secret beliefs have made themselves members of a cult.

Our scriptures and our history have left us with accounts of awesome priesthood power and spiritual manifestations. It should not be surprising that whisperings of great power would attract power hungry people wanting to partake of that power and have influence within the Church's organizations. Along with sincere Christians, the Church has attracted the power hungry and corrupt from the very beginning. I give my local leaders some slack because of the bad examples some of the General Authorities have set for them. We seem to have a problem in the Church in deciding whether to follow good advice from our leaders or imagine we have a better way. Some of our leaders have thought that they have a better idea than what is clearly taught in the Bible and Book of Mormon. The Book of Mormon predicts in 2nd Nephi 3:12 that it will grow together with the Bible "unto the confounding of false doctrines and laying down of contentions, and establishing peace among ..." the descendants of the Book of Mormon peoples.

When I think about bad examples Brigham Young comes to mind as the source of our racist doctrine. Those who drew up the announcement of the availability of the priesthood to men of all races ignored Brigham's influence. The suggestion, in the announcement, that it was consistent with the beliefs of the previous leaders of the Church on that subject was false. It was designed to encourage the Saints to overlook the fact that some of our prophets have tried to lead us astray. They tried to lead us astray when they previously said that the priesthood would never be available to black men of African descent during mortality. It was a lie which encouraged racism. When given the opportunity to acknowledge and reject that lie, those who announced the availability of the priesthood to men of all races chose to overlook it. Then they continued to provide lesson manuals which include that popular old teaching that God would not allow our prophet to lead us astray. Brigham Young himself proclaimed that he never said that he was going to be true to his God, JD Vol. 5, pp. 212-213. If we understand the Gospel and have the guidance of the Spirit we will not be led astray. Understanding the gospel requires a lot of prayerful study of the scriptures.

When David O. McKay was our prophet, some decades before the change, his efforts to receive revelation on the subject of African Blacks and the priesthood were not widely known. It was apparently his opinion that previous prophets had relied on doctrine that was not meant for our day, but merely a precedent from the past and the practice would change.

Since the priesthood was made available to men of all races we have no excuse for failing to believe in the equality of believers which has been a true principle at least since the crucifixion of Jesus. Under the Law of Moses the priesthood was available to only one tribe of the twelve, that is the tribe of Levi. However, when on rare occasions we are asked to name a favorite song to be sung by the congregation (we do this rarely) I sometimes hear the song, If I Could Hie to Kolob, called for which contains the phrase "there is no end to race". It may be my imagination, but when that phrase is sung I get the feeling as of something sinister lurking. I hope not, but I sometimes suspect that racist feelings are still interfering with our ability to enjoy the spirit and be inspired by the Holy Ghost. A persistent fascination with polygamy is, I fear, also doing harm to the ability of many of the brethren to be inspired by the Holy Ghost. They may find that they are inspired by the hope for power, authority, and many wives instead of guidance from God and a love of the Gospel.

Today a large majority of the Saints have not studied our history and scriptures in sufficient depth to know that our past leaders were given false doctrine because they desired it in accordance with Jacob 4:14. Jacob 4:14 tells us, and I'm paraphrasing, that the Jews were a stiff necked people who despised the words of plainness and sought for things which are hard to understand, therefore the Lord gave them things which were hard to understand that they might stumble. They fell into this problem because they chose to "look beyond the mark". In D&C 88:64-65 the warning in the Book of Mormon was renewed, but with different words,

64) "Whatsoever ye ask the Father in my name it shall be given unto you, that is expedient unto you.
65) And if ye ask anything that is no expedient for you, it shall turn unto your condemnation."

They do not understand that the Church was scourged from city to city because of their failures to live their religion and because of the false doctrine they desired.

Those who know that their favorite prophets taught that blacks would never hold the priesthood during mortality face some choices; They can choose to believe that their favorite prophets were right and that the change in policy was the result of political pressure much like when they had to give up polygamy, or they can choose to believe that Jacob 4:14 in the Book of Mormon was given to explain things which would happen to us in our day.

Those who believe the announcement's false report that the change was in accordance with the teachings of past prophets will find reassurance in the teaching that God will not allow his prophet to lead us astray. If they know that they have been misled and they keep their mouths shut about it their conscience will be seriously damaged. Those who need more convincing may listen to whisperings of things like, "If you are righteous enough the Lord will eventually ask you to do something which was formerly considered evil." This is the basis of secret doctrine within the Church. If they happen to come across testimony in the History of the Church that Joseph Smith took extra wives as early as 1831 they may believe it must have been alright for him to do it. This will encourage extreme authoritarian attitudes and they may find themselves willing to persecute anyone who disagrees with them. The desire for polygamy will likely become an obsession with them and they may find themselves unsympathetic towards those who have testimonies they deem inferior. If the brother having problems with his testimony has a wife who would be a real prize to be added to a Celestial harem that brother with an inferior testimony might find himself being pushed out of the Church by those who believe in secret doctrine.

As I have mentioned above, there are a few of the brethren in the Church who believe in secret doctrine which for them means that they are members of a cult of secrecy within the Church. I believe that most Latter-Day Saints are unaware of this. The only actual secret cults within the Church I have knowledge of are the fundamentalists or polygamists whose polygamist affiliation remains a secret. There needs to be some distinctions made between "secret cult' and "cult of secrecy". My meaning for "cult of secrecy" refers to those who believe that they could be asked to take extra wives at any time. It depends on how obsessed they are with polygamy just what it would take to get them to do it. About fifty years ago or so, there were people in a stake south of the Sacramento, California area who secretly became polygamists. I'm personally acquainted with a member who home taught a couple whose son-in-law joined the polygamists and was trying to get custody of their grandchild. He told me that those who could not afford the upkeep on extra wives allowed government welfare to take care of them. This way they could maintain their membership in the Church while they practiced polygamy in secret. The member I'm acquainted with was aware of eight polygamists rumored to have been discovered and excommunicated for apostasy. According to the rumor they all were members of a ward council or stake board.

I also have a friend whose brother is a polygamist and I recall a family member who conversed with a polygamist. The polygamist told him that when the Church renounced polygamy, one of the general authorities gave someone a special dispensation to keep the practice going. Brigham Young once predicted that "If it is wrong for a man to have more than one wife at a time, the Lord will reveal it by and by, and he will put it away that it will not be known in the Church." JD Vol. 11, p.268, Aug. 19, 1866. At least one of the general authorities took steps to insure that would not happen, if the rumor is correct.

Though it has been over a century since the practice of polygamy was abandoned by the Church we still lose members to the fundamentalists or polygamists. When expected additional changes to the definition of marriage are legalized, perhaps we will soon have another opportunity to show the Lord whether we believe the Book of Mormon with regard to its condemnation of polygamy. I see several possible reasons for the prophet Joseph Smith to have brought forth D&C 132, the revelation authorizing polygamy.

1.) I suspect section 132 was more than a test to see if we would be true to the Book of Mormon. I believe Joseph knew that the Saints had already been doomed to be driven out and their going against the Book of Mormon prohibition on plural marriage was to be a sign that they were unfit to settle the Center Place. Joseph knew that the other Christians and wicked people dwelling there would not allow a polygamous people to settle in the United States. How could they accept a doctrine so clearly rejected in the Book of Mormon? Jacob 2:24-28,

> 24) "Behold, David and Solomon truly had many wives and concubines, which thing was abominable before me, saith the Lord.
> 25) Wherefore, thus saith the Lord, I have led this people forth out of the land of Jerusalem, by the power of mine arm, that I might raise up unto me a righteous branch from the fruit of the loins of Joseph.
> 26) Wherefore, I the Lord God will not suffer that this people shall do like unto them of old.

> 27) Wherefore, my brethren, hear me, and hearken to the word of the Lord: For there shall not any man among you have save it be one wife; and concubines he shall have none;
> 28) For I, the Lord God, delight in the chastity of women. And whoredoms are an abomination before me; thus saith the Lord of Hosts."

2.) D&C 88:64-65,

> 64) "Whatsoever ye ask the Father in my name it shall be given unto you, that is expedient unto you.
> 65) And if ye ask anything that is no expedient for you, it shall turn unto your condemnation."

Jacob 4:14 and D&C 88:64-65 are my favorite answers for the existence of questionable doctrine in the Church. When the Lord's people despise the words of plainness He delivers things which are hard to understand to them so that they might stumble. D&C 132 is hard to understand. It is internally contradictory and contradicts the Bible and the Book of Mormon at least. Not only did it cause a lot of the saints to stumble, it caused them to be driven out of Nauvoo and it led to the death of Joseph Smith. Joseph Smith knew that destroying the print shop where the Nauvoo Expositor was printed would get him assassinated.

3.) Hard times were predicted by Isaiah for his people in Chapter 4:1 resulting in seven women taking hold of one man. For my part I hope that the predicted circumstances which made it seem necessary for seven women to take hold of one man in the distance past will not have to be repeated in the last days. If so I hope it was already fulfilled in the Utah Territory.

4.) With regard to the strong warnings in D&C 132 against refusing to be polygamists, I wonder if it's because the Lord, seeing that the greater number of women than men reaching the Utah territory would mean unnecessary suffering for them without polygamy. If that is the case then I suspect that the Lord knew it was necessary for Him to exaggerate the consequences of refusing to be polygamists in order for the sisters to agree to it. There is precedent for the Lord exaggerating. D&C 19 is interesting in that regard. Speaking of the day of judgment the Lord told Joseph in D&C 19,

> 4) "And every man must repent or suffer, for I, God, am endless.
> 5) Wherefore, I revoke not the judgments which I shall pass, but woes shall go forth, weeping, wailing and gnashing of teeth, yea, to those who are found on my left hand.
> 6) Nevertheless, it is not written that there shall be no end to this torment, but it is written endless torment.
> 7) Again, it is written eternal damnation; wherefore it is more express than other scriptures, that it might work upon the hearts of the children of men, altogether for my name's glory. ...
> 10) For, behold, the mystery of godliness, how great it is! For, behold, I am endless, and the punishment which is given from my hand is endless punishment, for Endless is my name. Wherefore-
> 11) Eternal punishment is God's punishment.
> 12) Endless punishment is God's punishment."

Upon a closer look at pertinent scriptures we find that those who must suffer for their own sins have only two possibilities, the telestial kingdom or perdition. Those who obtain the telestial kingdom have an end to their suffering, but not to the punishment, for they will never again enjoy the presence of the Father or Jesus, and that is endless punishment, and eternal punishment, or as Joseph Fielding Smith put it, eternal damnation, for they are prevented from advancing any further. We have no reason to believe that there is an end to suffering or punishment in Perdition.

The Savior explained to his disciples that there would be differing amounts of punishment, Luke 12:47-48. His followers on the old and new continents spoke only of eternal punishment for sinners and heaven for the righteous. The Book of Mormon warns us that there will be those who teach that it is alright to sin a little for God will beat us with a few stripes and everything will be alright, and that, I suspect, is what the Lord wanted to avoid. So God exaggerated on the duration of the suffering, but not on the duration of the punishment in the case of those who inherit the telestial Kingdom.

Section 132, however, adds additional complications to this scenario. It stipulates that those who have had their kingdoms sealed upon them can commit any sin except for the sin against the Holy Ghost and still obtain their kingdom (their exaltation) - very hard to understand. Brigham Young told the Saints that if a man found his brother in bed with his wife he should put a javelin through both of their hearts and they would be received into the kingdom of God, see JD Vol. 3 p.247. In Vol. 4, p.220 Brigham Young states, "I have known a great many men who have left this Church for whom there is no chance whatever for exaltation, but if their blood had been spilled, it would have been better for them." Yet in Vol. 1 of *DOCTRINES OF SALVATION*, in pp. 133-137, Joseph Fielding Smith declares Brigham's blood atonement to be little more than a penalty for certain kinds of evildoing. Joseph Fielding Smith takes five pages to assure us that in some cases the spilling of the blood of the guilty can have some undefined benefit. But, Brigham Young clearly presents blood atonement as a way of assuring that the sinner will go directly to his exaltation in some cases or at least receive some benefit in other cases.

In the above mentioned five pages, Joseph Fielding Smith declares the requirement that the Children of Israel wander in the wilderness for forty years until the older generation had died off was a case wherein the Lord had them slain by various methods so that they would not enter into the promised land. Actually, many of them died of old age or who would have raised the new generation.

The inclination to avoid owning up to the mistakes made by our past leaders will not serve us well when we need the Lord's intervention and we do now. In Leviticus 26:40-46 the Lord told the Children of Israel that He would remember his covenant with them when they confessed the sins of their fathers and accepted their punishment. Our leaders have not asked us to understand that the Lord gave us Brigham Young to tempt us with false doctrine because we had shown Him that we despised the words of plainness in the Book of Mormon and wanted instead things which are hard to understand. The Lord's determination to make certain that the Church will not fail its divine destiny does not prevent a few or most of us, including a few or most of our leaders from desiring to follow forbidden paths. Some of our past leaders have led us down paths which have brought the Church into disrepute. Whether they be few or many, the Lord will save the pure in heart even if it's only "one of a field".

Sometimes we forget that "it is not the work of God which is frustrated, but the work of man." The Lord is allowing the wheat and tares to grow together until the harvest as He told his followers during his earthly ministry, Matthew 13:24-30. The Lord is giving the tares a temporary reprieve and I don't resent his servants for allowing racists and those who long for polygamy to feel comfortable in the Church. But, I do resent the tares when they attempt to run any of us who disagree with them out of the Church. If we build up the Church by emboldening the tares among us then we are being set up to suffer much loss.

These last days are a time of restoration and of revealing of things hid up from the foundation of the world to come forth at this time. During Elijah's day, he called the children of Israel to repentance. What do we do when we hear that Elijah returned? Since he is spoken of as holding the keys to the sealing powers including the sealing of children to their parents, some assume that the temple in Jerusalem was used for the same purposes which our temples are used for today. What happened to things being revealed which had been hid from the foundation of the world to come forth in the last days? There is no thought that Elijah's performance of his duties during his mortal life may have earned him the right to reveal and bestow the keys to ordinances which have been hid up from the foundation of the world. Furthermore, Elijah's special talent for calling backsliding Israel to repentance may fall under the same general category as modern temple work as repentance is an essential ingredient in temple work also. God knows how to delegate and it seems rather silly to make assumptions about the reason God chose to delegate to someone.

That font we have in the basement of our temples which we use for baptism for the dead resembles a font in the temple which was in Jerusalem. The priests washed their burnt offerings in lavers and washed themselves in the font which they called a sea. We look forward to seeing the Jews accept the gospel, and yet some of us insist on trying to convince the world that everything we believe and practice was also practiced in every age of the earth's recorded history. That leaves no room for things which have been hid up from the foundation of the world to come forth in the latter days.

How often I have heard people saying that the Gospel being preached today was known to the prophets of all ages. And yet Jesus said to his apostles (Matthew 13:16 -17),

- 16) "But blessed are your eyes, for they see: and your ears, for they hear.
- 17) For verily I say unto you, That many prophets and righteous men have desired to see those things which ye see, and have not seen them; and to hear those things which ye hear, and have not heard them."

I never cease to be amazed by what passes for the truth. In the last few years I have heard High Priests in my stake teaching that the churches which teach that God is a spirit are preparing people to worship the Devil. Did he forget that our Doctrine and Covenants teaches that the Telestial Kingdom is presided over by the Holy Ghost? Did he forget that Jesus promised his followers that after he departed he would send the Holy Ghost and we know that the Holy Ghost is a personage of spirit? Substituting latter-day speculation for revealed truth is one sign of a cult.

When I came back to the church it soon became clear that some few of the saints had not forgiven me for turning my back on the church for twenty five years. When I came back I was just beginning to figure out a common lack of understanding about the details of the Lord's requirement that we forgive one another. Latter-Day Saints have a favorite scripture on forgiving which can be found in D&C 64:9, "Wherefore, I say unto you, that ye ought to forgive one another; for he that forgiveth not his brother his trespasses standeth condemned before the Lord; for there remaineth in him the greater sin."

I couldn't begin to count the number of times I have heard verse 9 quoted. On the other hand I don't recall ever hearing verse twelve quoted in recent years. D&C 64:12-13 reads,

> 12) And him that repenteth not of his sins, and confesseth them not, ye shall bring before the church, and do with him as the scripture saith unto you, either by commandment or by revelation."
> 13) And this ye shall do that God may be glorified-not because ye forgive not, having not compassion, but that ye may be justified in the eyes of the law, that ye may not offend him who is your lawgiver-"

Another cult-like danger we face comes from those who believe they have learned secrets by pondering the scriptures which go against the plain and simple teachings of the scriptures. People are complex and sometimes difficult to understand. I like to know what kind of God they worship and how they view reality and their place in it, but I don't like to judge them before I'm certain about such things. Truth be known, I prefer to avoid judging others. But, sooner or later we will find out what kind of God others worship and forewarned is forearmed. As soon they begin to imagine that they know the mysteries of God they will begin to think that their imagined mysteries supersede the things which are plainly taught in the scriptures. Alma 12:9-11,

> 9) And now Alma began to expound these things unto him, saying: It is given unto many to know the mysteries of god; nevertheless they are laid under a strict command that they shall not impart only according to the portion of his word which he doth grant unto the children of men, according to the heed and diligence which they give unto him.
> 10) And therefore, he that will harden his heart, the same receiveth the lesser portion of the word; and he that will not harden his heart, to him is given the greater portion of the word, until it is given him to know the mysteries of God until he knows them in full.
> 11) And they that will harden their hearts, to them is given the lesser portion of the word until they know nothing concerning his mysteries; and then they are taken captive by the devil, and led by his will down to destruction. Now this is what is meant by the chains of hell."

Those who obtain mysteries which they are not to impart to others don't obtain them by merely pondering. They obtain those mysteries from messengers sent by God, who warn them against imparting those mysteries to others. The Book of Mormon as we now have it contains lesser amounts of information than is available in the untranslated plates. It also contains less of the mysteries. Those who falsely believe that they know the mysteries of God will not be privy to the real mysteries. The real mysteries will become will-o'-the-wisps which distracts them from the lesser things which are contained in our scriptures. We are told that we will not be given the full account until we believe the lesser things. Tell me how that works; how are we to believe what the Book of Mormon says against polygamy if we believe we have been given some greater thing, some mystery which supersedes the Book of Mormon teachings against polygamy? How are we going to understand the greater things or even the lesser things while our minds are full of the desire for many wives? If we are deceived about the mysteries then we will find that we cannot even understand the lesser things or believe them.

The longing for polygamy and/or racist feelings, I suspect, are entertained by those scholars and leaders who are familiar with the cover-ups of our history and they are participating in those cover-ups. Perhaps they imagine that those things they are covering up are great mysteries which they are not allowed to impart to us so they perpetuate the lies at the risk of their own souls.

The prophet who condensed the histories on the plates which were translated into the Book of Mormon wanted us to know that the Lord was angry with the Children of Israel because they didn't understand the mercies of God. Alma 33:16, "For behold, he said: Thou art angry, oh Lord, with this people, because they will not understand thy mercies which thou hast bestowed upon them because of thy Son."

There has been some confusion in the world about who is capable of sin. It is spoken of in the Book of Mormon as well as in the Bible. Mosiah 3 in the Book of Mormon speaks of it quite clearly.

> 22) And even at this time, when thou shalt have taught thy people the things which the Lord thy God hath commanded thee, even

then are they found no more blameless in the sight of God, only according to the words which I have spoken unto thee."

Jesus also taught this principle during his mortal ministry. John 15:22, "If I had not come and spoken unto them, they had not had sin: But now they have no cloke for their sin."

So, why do we do baptisms for the dead? Because when the gospel is preached to the spirits in prison their knowledge of the evil residing in their hearts will need to be repented of and create the desire in them to be baptized for the remission of those sinful thoughts.

There have also been efforts to minimize the effectiveness of repentance when it comes to sex sin. It's easy to get caught up in such things. I don't recall whether I immediately recognized the falseness of the comparison which was made to the pulling out of a nail from a board, "it leaves a scar" they said. A more appropriate comparison was made to the erasing of the record of our sins from the pages of the Book of Life. The false idea that forgiveness of sin was like pulling a nail from a board which leaves a scar was becoming so popular that one of our leaders explained that it was as though sins were kept in a card file and when they were forgiven the Lord removed the card from the persons file and placed it in his own personal file showing that he now owned that sin and had already paid for it. He paid for it on the cross where he paid for all the sins of those who properly repent.

The reason I became interested in the Mormon Church was because the protestant church I belonged to took the rigid stance that everyone who failed to become a saved Christian in mortality was bound for an eternity in hell. The Christian churches tend to take extreme stands on the matter of salvation. While some have almost everyone going to hell, others have hardly anyone going there.

Because of their failure to take the Book of Mormon seriously enough many Latter-Day Saints believe that the number of people who have come to earth and obtained a body but will not inherit a kingdom of glory can be numbered on the fingers of one hand. Their justification comes from someone (Joseph Smith I believe) saying that in order to become a Son of Perdition you must have been given the power of God during your earth life and turned against God. They forget the passage which says in D&C 88:31-33;

> 31) And also they who are quickened by a portion of the telestial glory shall then receive of the same, even a fullness.
> 32) And they who remain shall also be quickened; nevertheless, they shall return again to their own place, to enjoy that which they are willing to receive, because they were not willing to enjoy that which they might have received."
> 33) For what doth it profit a man if a gift is bestowed upon him, and he receive not the gift? Behold, he rejoices not in that which is given unto him, neither rejoices in him who is the giver of the gift."

False doctrine in the Church is a mixture of oversimplifications and despising the words of plainness in favor of unnecessarily complex doctrine. When Joseph Smith spoke of people in mortality who became Sons of Perdition he was referring to those who had sinned against the greater light to such extent that they had no possibility of escaping Hell, their fate was sealed. They are a very special and limited case, but not the only way for people to be consigned to Perdition. All the rest of those who do not repent in time to escape having to suffer for their sins in Hell until the final judgment have the possibility of obtaining the telestial Kingdom if they can abide the law of a telestial kingdom and if they want to abide the law of a telestial kingdom, but they are not guaranteed telestial glory. See D&C 88:24,

> 24) And he who cannot abide the law of a telestial kingdom cannot abide a telestial glory; therefore he is not meet for a kingdom of glory. Therefore he must abide a kingdom which is not a kingdom of glory."

The above is just one example of things which show that we as Latter-Day Saints need to be more faithful in studying the scriptures. You don't get to escape eternity in the outer darkness of Hell merely because you didn't become a Son of Perdition during mortality. You also must be shut up in hell until the final judgment and become capable and desirous of living the law of the telestial Kingdom and want to be there. Just what is meant by a "kingdom which is not a kingdom of glory" might leave a little wiggle room for something other than outer darkness with the Devil and his angels, but to me the lack of glory indicates darkness and it will for me until more light is shed on the subject.

To my way of thinking there is also enough confusion about Abraham in the Church to qualify some of us as belonging to a cult of Abraham. Some of that confusion comes from reading the Book of Abraham in our Pearl of Great Price. As I've stated before, my testimony does not require me to believe that the Pearl of Great Price is completely credible. I don't know whether to consider it apocryphal, the pure word of God, or just something which is hard to understand. Whatever the case I do consider it hard to understand and the very kind of thing the Lord would give to a people who did not have proper respect for the plain and simple gospel revealed in the Book of Mormon. Jacob 4:14 seems to me like a perfect fit for the Pearl of Great Price and in the following paragraphs I will reveal my reasons for thinking so. As a comparison, let us examine the information about Melchizedek and Abraham.

Melchizedek was a king over the land of Salem (Alma 13:17) which was full of wickedness and abominations, but he received the office of the high priesthood according to the holy order of God and preached repentance unto his people. He established peace in the land in his day thus he was called the prince of peace - there were none greater. A study of the thirteenth chapter of Alma will show that obtaining the high priesthood is about righteousness, not lineage. In the Book of Abraham, even the information about lineage is very confusing.

The Book of Abraham is said to have been translated by Joseph Smith, from a history written by Abraham upon papyrus. In chapter 1:2 Abraham speaks of his desire to possess greater knowledge, be a father of nations, a prince of peace, and tells of his success in that quest "I became a rightful heir, a High Priest, holding the right belonging to the fathers." But he gives no details as to how he was ordained. In Abraham's day, it was Melchizedek who became a High Priest. Abraham's blessings were about earthly blessings for mortality and fame along with a large posterity in the future wherein all who accept the gospel will be accounted his seed in the last days. Abraham was also promised an everlasting inheritance. The Book of Abraham goes on to tell us that Abraham was blessed by Jehovah when He appeared to him, in chapter 2:9-11,

> (9) "And I will make of thee a great nation, and I will bless thee above all measure, and I will make thy name great among all nations, and thou shalt be a blessing unto thy seed after thee, that in their hands they shall bear this ministry and Priesthood unto all nations;
> (10) And I will bless them through thy name; for as many as receive this Gospel shall be called after thy name, and shall be accounted thy seed, and shall rise up and bless thee, as their father;
> (11) And I will bless them that bless thee, and curse them that curse thee; ... for I give unto thee a promise that ... in thy seed after thee ... shall all the families of the earth be blessed, even with the blessings of the Gospel, which are the blessings of salvation, even of life eternal."

The Book of Abraham also tells of Pharaoh ruling Egypt, he being the eldest son of Egyptus. This Egyptus was the daughter of Egyptus and Ham. Chapter 1:23-24 tells us that Egypt "signifies that which is forbidden ... thus from Ham, sprang that race which preserved the curse in the land." The intent here seems to be to associate Ham with a pre-flood curse. However, Pharaoh, the eldest son of the younger Egyptus, was blessed of Noah "with the blessings of the earth (Cain's curse stipulated that the earth would not yield up its strength for him), and with the blessings of wisdom, but cursed him as pertaining to the priesthood.", (Abraham 1:26). If however, Pharaoh was blessed with the blessings of the earth and wisdom that would seem to counteract the curse of being a slave. According to Genesis 9:25, Canaan was cursed by Noah. However, Canaan was the son of Ham through whom the curse in the land was preserved. Yet it was Canaan and not other sons of Ham whom Noah cursed to become a servant unto his brethren.

Additionally, according to the inspired version of the Bible, Canaan was told (Gen. 9:30) that a veil of darkness would cover him that he might be known among all men. Somehow, according to the Book of Abraham, (1:21-22) the;

> (21) ...King of Egypt was a descendant from the loins of Ham, and was a partaker of the blood of the Canaanites by birth.
> (22) From this descent sprang all the Egyptians, and thus the blood of the Canaanites were preserved in the land."

It isn't clear how Pharaoh was descended from Canaan, but it is clear from the HC that although the prophet Joseph Smith did refer to the blacks as the seed of Cain, Joseph Smith viewed the slaves as suffering under the curse Noah placed on Canaan. It appears to me that the Book of Abraham is so confusing about the curses that it may have been something other than what it claimed to be for Joseph ignored the attempt therein to associate the fate of the seed of Canaan with a pre-flood curse, (HC Vol. 2 p.438). Some of the later general authorities of the church associate Ham's descendants with the curse of Cain.

As to the priesthood which Pharaoh was banned from, in the Joseph Smith Inspired Version of the Bible we find in Genesis 14:27-32 a description of the priesthood given the ancient patriarchs. Before describing this priesthood the manner of delivery is described,

> (29) "And it was delivered unto men by the calling of his own voice, according to his own will, unto as many as believed on his name."

After describing the great power these High Priests held it says,
> (32) "And men having this faith, coming up unto this order of God, were translated and taken up into heaven.
> (33) And now, Melchizedek was a priest of this order, therefore he obtained peace in Salem, and was called the Prince of peace.
> (34) And his people wrought righteousness, and obtained heaven, and sought for the city of Enoch which God had before taken, separating it from the earth, having reserved it unto the latter days, or the end of the world."

In verse 37 it says that Melchizedek blessed Abram without mentioning that he was given the priesthood. In chapter 15:18 the Lord tells Abram that he will die and be buried in a good old age.

For all of the praise Abraham has received he was not numbered among those who rated being translated into heaven without dying. That Abraham received such high praise may be seen as saying more about God than about Abraham. God loves to honor those who seek him and are not ashamed of being known as one who wants to please him even if they fall short of being worthy of translation. God had something else in store for Abraham which may have been merely a consolation prize, but was a great honor worthy of someone who was recognized as a friend of God.

We find in D&C 84:14 that Abraham was ordained by Melchizedek, but, it does not say that he was given a promise of being translated for he was told in Genesis that he would die at a good old age. When Melchizedek was taken up Abraham was left behind to produce a numerous offspring while living among a people who were not a Zion people.

In D&C 84:42 on September 22nd, 1832. those who were assembled were told that their priesthood was "confirmed by mine own voice out of the heavens; and even I have given the heavenly hosts and mine angels charge concerning you."

When the twelve apostles were chosen in February of 1835 they were told by Oliver Cowdery of the First Presidency (History of the Church Vol. II, pp. 195-196) "... but it is necessary that you receive a testimony from heaven for yourselves; so that you can bear testimony to the truth of the book of Mormon, and that you have seen the face of God. ... Your ordination is not full and complete till God has laid His hand upon you."

From the parable of the wheat and tares we learn that in the last days we are to live among the wicked (in the world and in the church?). Paul thought that they were in the last days and he said, 1Cor. 11:19, "For there must also be heresies among you, that they which are approved may be made manifest among you." And yet we love to ignore the warning in the Book of Mormon against promoting the idea that "All is well in Zion, yea Zion prospereth." We love to dig up heresies out of conference talks or the vain imaginings of our mystery loving friends, things which are clearly proclaimed against in holy writ, and pass them off as gospel.

Recently someone who has done a lot of reading in doctrine came up with a chart which shows three Grand Orders of the Melchizedek Priesthood, but shows the Patriarchal Order as being superior to the Melchizedek Priesthood. Joseph Smith did not teach that the Patriarchal Order was superior to the Melchizedek Priesthood. He listed it as being between the Melchizedek and Levitical Priesthoods. H.C. vol. 5, pp.554 & 555,

The 1st The King of Shiloam, (Salem) [Melchizedek] had power and authority over that of Abraham, holding the key and the power of endless life. ... Those holding the fullness of the Melchizedek Priesthood are kings and priests of the Most High God, holding the keys of power and blessings. In fact, that priesthood is a perfect law of theocracy, ... administering endless lives to the sons and daughters of Adam. ...

The 2nd Priesthood is Patriarchal authority. ...

The 3rd is what is called the Levitical Priesthood,..."

Joseph Smith was differentiating between the power and authority held by Melchizedek and that held by Abraham without really telling us much about the Patriarchal Order. It appears to me that the great patriarchs of the Old Testament held the fullness of the Melchizedek Priesthood, meaning they had the keys to exercise the priesthood in its fullness while Abraham was merely a member of the patriarchal order having little more in the way of keys than the authority to pass it on to his progeny.

Melchizedek had the power to secure peace and take his people up to God as did Enoch. Abraham had some portion of the Melchizedek Priesthood, but did not have the assignment (keys) or power to establish peace and take his people up to God as did Melchizedek. Other High Priests who were sufficiently righteous were taken up to heaven. Some, such as Elijah and possibly Moses were taken alone. In Gen. 7:33-34 of the inspired version Enoch beheld the Holy Ghost fall on many, "and they were caught up by the powers of heaven into Zion." Abraham had no such promise. Abraham's assignment was to live among the worldly and have a numerous posterity, be the father of nations, and die and be buried at an old age. He lived among people who lived a lesser law which did not give them any hope of eternal life, just as the Law of Moses did not give the children of Israel any promise of eternal life. The Children of Israel were allowed to have more than one wife as was Abraham.

Abraham had wives and concubines, but through Sara came the children of the promise. Romans 9:7-9,

> (7) "Neither, because they are the seed of Abraham, are they all children: but, in Isaac shall thy seed be called.
> (8) That is, they which are the children of the flesh, these are not the children of God: but the children of the promise are counted for the seed.
> (9) For this is the word of promise, at this time will I come, and Sara shall have a son."

Out of respect for Abraham's love for his son Ishmael, God promised to make Ishmael fruitful in Genesis 17:20, but He reaffirmed in verse 21, "But my covenant will I establish with Isaac". So we see that Abraham's polygamous progeny did not figure in God's plans to bless all the families of the earth by Abraham's seed.

Abraham's polygamous progeny were not included in the covenant God made with Abraham. And yet, the section on polygamy (D&C 132) says that Abraham's progeny through Hagar "was fulfilling, among other things, the promises". It also commands us to do the works of Abraham. See D&C 132:32-35;

> 32) "Go ye, therefore, and do the works of Abraham; enter ye into my law and ye shall be saved.
> 33) But if ye enter not into my law ye cannot receive the promise of my father, which he made unto Abraham.
> 34) God commanded Abraham, and Sarah gave Hagar to Abraham to wife. And why did she do it? Because this was the law; and from Hagar sprang many people. This therefore, was fulfilling, among other things, the promises.
> 35) Was Abraham, therefore under condemnation? Verily I say unto you, nay; for I, the Lord, commanded it."

Jacob's polygamous progeny were included in the covenant. It was because of Jacob's father-in-law's trickery that he married sisters. It was at his wives insistence that he received additional wives. Abraham, on the other hand, obtained most of his wives and concubines after Sarah's death, and none of his extra wives and concubines and their offspring had anything to do with the promises. Adding the above verses to other references about Abraham makes the section on polygamy very hard to understand.

While Melchizedek obtained peace and sought for the City of Enoch, Abraham received promises about the distant future, Hebrews 11:9-13.

> (9) "By faith he sojourned in the land of promise, as in a strange country, dwelling in tabernacles with Isaac and Jacob, the heirs with him of the same promise:
> (10) For he looked for a city which hath foundations, whose builder and maker is God.
> (11) Through faith also Sara herself received strength to conceive seed, and was delivered of a child when she was past age, because she judged him faithful who had promised.
> (12) Therefore sprang there even of one, and him as good as dead, so many as the stars of the sky in multitude, and as the sand which is by the sea shore innumerable.
> (13) These all died in faith, not having received the promises, but having seen them afar off, and were persuaded of them, and embraced them, and confessed that they were strangers and pilgrims on the earth."

We are living in a day when the keys of every dispensation have been restored. Thus, though we live at a time when we are to remain on the earth to establish a numerous posterity as did Abraham, we also have temple ordinances whereby we may be sealed up unto eternal life. The Church being fully organized at this time, we have three priesthood offices which are organized into quorums which are equal in authority to preside over the affairs of whole Church, the Seventy, the Apostles and the First Presidency. The quorums of Elders and High Priests only have local authority. Likewise, of course, the Aaronic Priesthood.

It appears to me that the chart has it's roots in the days of polygamy in Utah for the main feature listed on the chart for the Patriarchal Order is the "new and everlasting covenant of marriage" which can be taken as code for polygamy in D&C 132. I suspect that the chart is meant to make Abraham's priesthood appear to be superior to Melchizedek's in order to give polygamous heretics a proselyting tool. It is at least designed to draw our minds away from the condemnation of polygamy in the Book of Mormon.

It is interesting to note that those who succeeded in calling a people to repentance and taking them along when they were taken up to God without tasting death also left a posterity behind to continue their blood line. Enoch, for instance was the great grandfather of Noah. He therefore had a more numerous posterity than did Abraham (one of his descendants), plus he was taken to God without tasting death. In the Inspired text quoted above (Genesis 14:34) it can be seen that Enoch and his city were translated. Also of interest is the account of Abram being blest by Melchizedek in the Book of Jasher, chapter 16:11. In this account Melchizedek is called Adonizedek and is said to actually be Shem, one of Abraham's ancestors and the son of Noah. Thus Melchizedek may also be a High Priest who has a numerous posterity as well as being one of those who didn't taste of death.

We must face the fact that as a church we contributed to racism and the Pearl of Great Price was used to promote it. In spite of the fact that the New Testament, the Book of Mormon, and the Doctrine and Covenants stood up for the equality of believers the Church held on to the practice of withholding the priesthood from blacks of African descent until 1978. In D&C 38:25-27 the Lord told Joseph Smith that He was like a man who had twelve sons who served him well, He could not consider himself just if he told one of them to set over there dressed in rags and told another to set over here dressed in robes.

We can also look to the Old Testament wherein Isaiah saw the day (chapter 56:3-7) when all people, even the eunuchs and the stranger would have a place within his house which would be open to all who take hold of his covenant and keep the Sabbath. We are living in that day, for our temples have no restrictions regarding national origin or physical perfection. The stain of racism was so prevalent in the earth that the Lord in his mercy waited for over one hundred years before requiring his people to bring the faithful men of all races into the priesthood.

How long will the Lord wait for his people to understand atonement? Mosiah 15 explains redemption in simple terms. The redeemed are the seed of Jesus which includes all the holy prophets and those who have harkened unto their words. Those who sinned without a knowledge of the gospel are also redeemed by the Lord according to verses 24 and 25. Brigham thought that the seed of Jesus were the offspring and descendants of the Savior's polygamous marriages.

www.ingramcontent.com/pod-product-compliance
Lightning Source LLC
Chambersburg PA
CBHW030114100526
44591CB00009B/404